Walk, Amble, Stroll

Vocabulary Building Through Domains
Level 2

Kathryn Trump
Sherry Trechter
Dee Ann Holisky

All of George Mason University

Heinle & Heinle Publishers
A Division of Wadsworth, Inc.
Boston, Massachusetts 02116 USA

For Gena. (D.H.)

For Iris and other future language learners. (S.T.)

For Ray and Verna Gallmeier and my four boys. (K.T.)

Publisher: Stanley J. Galek

Editorial Director: David C. Lee

Editorial Production Manager: Elizabeth Holthaus

Manufacturing Coordinator: Lisa McLaughlin

Project Management: Elm Street Publications

Design and Production: PC&F, Inc.

Illustrations: Dave Blanchette

Cover Illustration: Giacomo Balla. *Dynamism of a Dog on a Leash.* Oil on canvas, $35^3/8$ x $43^1/4$. The Albright-Knox Art Gallery, Bequest of A. Conger Goodyear and Gift of George F. Goodyear, 1964.

Text and Cartoon Credits: p.40, John Flinn, "Researchers Found Laughter to be a Powerful Medicine." Reprinted with permission from the San Francisco Examiner. © 1991 San Francisco Examiner; pp.46 and 150, "Marvin," reprinted with special permission of North America Syndicate; p.129, realia courtesy of Fairfax Hospital, Falls Church, VA; p.63, "Calvin and Hobbes" and p.125, "For Better or for Worse," copyright 1986 Universal Press Syndicate. Reprinted with permission. All rights reserved.

Photo Credits: p.49, Archive Photos; p.50, Peter Menzel; p.53, J. Walter Thompson Co.; p.55, Spencer Grant from Monkmeyer Press Photo Service; p.56, Russ Kinne, Comstock; p.73, *(left)* Jeff Greenberg, *(right)* Archive Photos/Lambert; p.117, Associated Press Photo; p.128, *(left)* Archive Photos, *(right)* Archive Photos/Watson; p.152, Sven Martson, Comstock; pg.160, Archive Photos, R. Gates; p.161, Peter Menzel.

Heinle & Heinle is a division of Wadsworth, Inc.

Manufactured in the United States of America.

ISBN: 0-8384-2280-2

10 9 8 7 6 5 4

Table of Contents

To the Student

Are you tired?

Exhausted?

Worn-out?

Is this how you feel some days after you have spent hours and hours trying to learn new words in English? You already know many words, but you probably feel that you never know enough. You always need to know more.

Sometimes words are easy to learn because they are similar to words in your language (such as radio or computer). Other words are easy to learn because they are part of the basic vocabulary of English (such as student or love). However, the work gets harder when you go beyond this basic vocabulary. We have written this book to help you learn words beyond the basic vocabulary.

The idea for this book started with an ESL teacher who was looking for a way to help students learn new words. One day, she taught her students ten different words for the basic word walk. They learned the words quickly and remembered them well—and they had fun studying them too!

The teacher was pleased and that first group of related words became the basis for this book, *Walk, Amble, Stroll*. The most important thing about this book is the way the words are grouped. They are organized into word domains and each unit has one or more domains. A domain is a group of words that are all related to one basic idea. A good example is the WALK domain which contains words that have a similar meaning to walk. Walk is a word that you know. Here are two other words that mean walk:

amble   stroll

The words amble and stroll add meaning to the word walk. They mean to walk slowly with no goal in mind. In the first chapter of this book, you'll learn many other words that add extra meaning to the basic idea of walk.

There's one thing we want you to remember as you go through this book: when you first look at a domain, there will be many words that are new to you, but don't worry. In each domain there will also be some words that you already know. That's good! These words will help you learn and remember the words that you don't know. The more you see these familiar and unfamiliar words together, the more comfortable and confident you will feel with them.

Using domains to learn vocabulary can help you:

- attach many new words to one basic word that you already know
- recognize the words the next time you see them in writing
- put more words in your active vocabulary; you will know what these words mean and you will be able to use them in speaking and writing

Learning vocabulary is an important step to better language skills. You know that and we do too. We have written this book to help you learn new vocabulary quickly and remember it easily. We also hope you will have some fun with the words!

To the Teacher

Walk, Amble, Stroll: Vocabulary Building Through Domains is an intermediate-level textbook for students who are ready to expand their vocabulary beyond the basic level. It can be used in a class devoted to vocabulary building or as a supplementary text in a reading, writing, or integrated skills class. It can also be used for self-study by individual students.

Rapid and continual vocabulary expansion is critical for students learning English as a second or foreign language. Our goal in writing this book was to provide intermediate-level students with an efficient and enjoyable way to expand their vocabularies. We introduce vocabulary through a concept and teach words that are related to that concept. We call this group of related words a "domain." This focus on concepts and word domains lends itself to a rich variety of activities that appeal to students with different learning styles.

I. Major Features of this Approach

1. Words are easier to learn when they are connected in some way. Through domains, students can earn a larger number of words more quickly.

2. The words are reinforced by a developmental progression of exercises, moving from the simple to the more complex and open-ended. Students gradually move from beginning practice with the words into creating their own contexts for the words.

3. The students can build on familiar concepts. They aren't overwhelmed by learning large numbers of new words because they already know some of the words in each domain.

4. Charts (not word lists) are used to display the words. These aid the students in visualizing the domains and remembering them.

5. Students are learning a technique that they can use with other concepts and with new words as they come up. Teachers can also use this technique to teach other words as they come up in the classroom.

II. Format of Each Unit

Each unit follows a similar format and contains the sections below.

1. Getting Ready. This section consists of a few questions to help the student focus on both the concept and the dimensions of the domain.

2. Introducing the Domain. The words in the domain are introduced in a brief narrative and then they are presented in a chart. The chart is designed to reflect the important dimensions of the domain.

3. Exploring the Domain. In most of the units, this section contains a narrative that uses the words in context.

4. Exercises. A progression of exercises provides the students with practice using the words in a variety of ways. The exercise progression has three steps: **(a)** The first step involves manipulative exercises that familiarize the student with the words. These are helpful for short-term memory. **(b)** The second step consists of two-step, problem-solving exercises. These exercises don't focus on the words themselves, but instead require the student to take a second step, from the word to its meaning within a specific context. These exercises ensure that the words will be stored in long-term memory. **(c)** The last step consists of open-ended communicative activities for writing or discussion. At this point, the students are ready to use the words to talk about their own experiences.

5. Expanding the Domain. This is an optional section at the end of most units. It introduces additional vocabulary that is related to the words in the domain or presents extended uses for the words. In some chapters, we ask students to bring in new words that belong in the domain.

III. How to Use This Book

1. The order of presentation. The units in this book do not have to be covered in order. However, we recommend starting with the first three or four units, because the concept of domains is introduced and most major exercise types are presented. After that, teachers can follow the order of the book or choose chapters that tie in with their curriculum.

2. Teaching speed. Students using this book tend to learn words more quickly than they do using other vocabulary materials. This is because of the organization of vocabulary around a familiar concept and the psycholinguistic reality of word domains.

3. Using dictionaries and thesauruses. We encourage the use of dictionaries, both bilingual and English-English. The domain charts will provide students with a clear idea of the meaning of the word from the way it's placed on the chart. However, some students might find that using a dictionary will clarify the meaning of the word. In addition, teachers who want to introduce the use of a thesaurus will find that the domain concept enhances its use as a resource tool.

4. Other activities. We hope that you will expand on the units in the book by creating games, supplementary materials and other activities for your students. We also hope that you will encourage them to bring in examples of words from domains in new contexts that they have found in their everyday lives.

It has been exciting for us to see other teachers use these materials and design their own activities. You can be as creative, imaginative, inventive, and ingenious as you want to be!

IV. Resources for the Teacher

If you are interested in finding out more about vocabulary learning and teaching, here are some references that we have found helpful.

Aitchison, Jean. *Words in the Mind: An Introduction to the Mental Lexicon*. Oxford: Basil Blackwell, 1987.

Carter, Ronald and Michael McCarthy, eds. *Vocabulary and Language Teaching*. London: Longman, 1988.

Cruse, D.A. *Lexical Semantics*. Cambridge: Cambridge University Press, 1986.

Curtis, Mary E. and Margaret G. McKeown, eds. *The Nature of Vocabulary Acquisition*. Hillsdale, New Jersey: Lawrence Erlbaum Associates, 1987.

McCarthy, Michael. *Vocabulary*. Oxford: Oxford University Press, 1990.

Nagy, William. *Teaching Vocabulary to Improve Reading Comprehension*. Urbana, Illinois: National Council of Teachers of English, 1988.

Nation, I.S.P. *Teaching and Learning Vocabulary*. New York: Newbury House, 1990.

Acknowledgments

Walk, Amble, Stroll: Vocabulary Building Through Domains emerged from a semantics class taught by Dr. Dee Ann Holisky at George Mason University in 1982. We would like to thank the members of that class who became convinced that the concept of semantic fields, or domains, could be used to teach vocabulary. The students of the English Language Institute at George Mason University further convinced us that this method works through their enthusiasm for this new way of learning vocabulary.

We have benefitted from the work of other professionals, especially George Miller, Christine Fellbaum and William Nagy. We are also indebted to the teachers who piloted the chapters (Mary Jane Saunders, Enrica Frost, Susan Klingaman, David Coia, and Judy Graves and the staff at Eurocentre in Alexandria, Virginia). We would like to thank Marshall Kolin, Phyllis Duryee, Melissa Allen, Sandy Sklarew, and Mei-Ling Huang. Thanks also go to the following reviewers: Bill Biddle, Audrey Blackwell, Maryanne Kearny-Datesman, Gail Kellersberger, John Kopec, Mr. Nakai, and Anca Menoianu. Finally, we want to acknowledge our editor, David Lee, who has been a responsive, enthusiastic partner in the writing of this book and Harriet Dishman for her caring and careful attention to detail.

K.T.
S.T.
D.H.

UNIT I

A Giant Step To Vocabulary Building

THE WALK DOMAIN

I. Getting Ready

Words, words, and more words! There are more than half a million words in the English language. It isn't surprising that many students think it is difficult to develop a good vocabulary in English.

Discuss the following questions either with your whole class or in a small group.

1. How do you feel about learning new words? Do you like it or do you think it's boring?

2. When you are reading in English and you find a word that you don't know, what do you do? Do you:
   –look the word up in your dictionary?
   –ask a friend what it means?
   –guess at its meaning?
   –ignore it?

3. Do you think it is important to build up your English vocabulary? Why?

II. Introducing Word Domains

The units in this book will help you improve your vocabulary quickly and easily. Each unit has one or more groups of words followed by paragraphs to help you understand the new words. There are also exercises to help you learn the new words.

This book is different from other vocabulary books because of the way the words have been divided into groups. In each unit you will find a group of words that are similar in meaning. This collection of words is called a "domain." Take a few minutes to look over the domain for the verb walk. Mark any words that you don't know.

The WALK Domain

No Goal	Step		Attitude		Speed
Aimless	**Even**		**Secret**		**Slow**
wander	march	pace	prowl	slink	inch
stroll			sneak	steal	creep
saunter	**Light**				edge
roam	tiptoe		**Proud**		
amble			strut	swagger	**Fast**
ramble	**Heavy**				hasten
	plod	trudge	**Confident**		hurry
			stride		
	Unsteady				
	waddle	toddle	**Sad**		
	stagger	falter	shuffle	slouch	
	stumble				
	hobble	limp			

Most of the domains in this book have one or two general words. The most general word in this domain is walk. We call this domain the WALK domain.

All the other words in this domain have the same basic meaning as walk. But each word has some additional meaning as well. For instance, wander means to walk with no goal in mind. March means to walk with an even step, like a soldier in a parade. Although wander and march have the same basic meaning as walk, they both describe a special way of walking.

When we use a word that has more meaning than the basic word, we give more information. Compare the two sentences below.

1. The children walked home from school.
2. The children wandered home from school.

Both sentences have the same basic meaning, but the second sentence gives more information than the first one. The second sentence tells us that the children walked in a slow, aimless way. They didn't go directly home. Maybe they crossed the street to talk to a friend or look in the window of a store.

III. Exploring the Domain

A. A number of verbs in the WALK domain mean to walk aimlessly, with no goal in mind. You might stroll or saunter through a park on a nice sunny day when you have nothing important to do. Have you ever wandered through an airport for an hour while you were waiting for your flight? Sometimes children amble or ramble on the way home from school. They walk slowly, stopping to look at things, and perhaps they take the long way home. If you lost your pet dog or cat, you might roam the streets for hours looking for it.

wander
stroll
saunter
roam
amble
ramble

B. When we walk, we take steps. Some verbs in the WALK domain tell us about the kind of steps someone is taking. Have you ever seen a lion walking back and forth in his cage? We say he is pacing. When you pace or march, you walk with an even step. Soldiers march and people in a parade march. When soldiers are walking in thick, heavy mud, they can't march. They plod or trudge. The mud sticks to their boots and makes it hard for them to walk. We also use plod and trudge to show that someone is unhappy or tired. Do you ever plod to class?

march
pace
tiptoe
plod
trudge

If your step is light and you walk on your toes, you tiptoe. Sometimes we tiptoe when we don't want to be heard.

C. Sometimes we walk with an unsteady step. There are seven verbs in the WALK domain that describe this kind of walking. The chart on page 4 will help you understand them.

Walk—Unsteady Step

toddle to walk like a small child

waddle to walk like a duck

stagger
falter } to walk in a clumsy, uneven way
stumble

hobble } to walk like someone with
limp } an injured foot

D. Some verbs tell us about the attitude of the person who is walking. For example, a thief doesn't want anyone to see or hear him. He might prowl or slink through a dark, empty house. If a child wants to surprise her father, she might sneak up behind him and yell, "Boo!" If teenagers don't want their parents to know they are going out, they might steal quietly out of the house.

> prowl
> slink
> sneak
> steal
>
> strut
> swagger
>
> stride
>
> shuffle
> slouch

The verb stride expresses a different attitude. When a singer strides onto the stage, she gives us the idea that she is feeling confident and sure of herself. People who are feeling very proud might strut or swagger. They walk with their heads up and their shoulders back. When they strut or swagger, they give the idea that they think they are better than everyone else.

The last two verbs, shuffle and slouch, indicate that the person who is walking is sad. When a man shuffles, he drags his feet as he walks, making noise as his feet move across the floor. If a woman slouches into the room, she walks with her head and shoulders down. Her posture shows that she is sad. A child who has just failed a test might slouch or shuffle home to tell his parents about it.

E. There are five verbs that tell us about the speed at which someone or something is walking. Have you ever tried to move through a crowded room? You probably had to edge your way across the room. Have you ever watched a cat inch or creep toward a bird? The cat moves slowly and carefully. But a hungry cat will hasten or hurry to its food dish when someone puts food in it. Would you creep or hasten if you were walking on an icy sidewalk? Do you hurry or inch your way to class when you are late?

> inch
> creep
> edge
>
> hasten
> hurry

IV. Learning the Words

While you are doing the following exercises, try to remember this: *You don't have to memorize the exact meaning of every word!*

By the end of this unit, you should know the general meaning of each word in the WALK domain. You should be able to connect the new word to the basic word walk. When you see or hear the word plod, you should remember that it means a way of walking. If you also remember that it means to walk with a heavy step, the way a person walks in mud, that's even better! But you will usually understand the meaning of the sentence just by knowing that plod means a kind of walking.

V. Exercises

Exercise 1: Beginning Practice

Cross out the word that doesn't belong.

Example: stagger   ~~swagger~~   stumble   falter

1. pace   falter   march
2. plod   tiptoe   trudge
3. stride   waddle   limp
4. inch   march   creep   edge
5. wander   roam   amble   hasten
6. slink   slouch   sneak   steal

Exercise 2: More Practice

At the beginning of this unit, you learned that all the verbs in the WALK domain have the same basic meaning as <u>walk</u>. But remember that each verb has some extra meaning as well. Think about this extra meaning as you do the exercise below.

Part A

Write *NG* if the verb means to walk with *no goal*. Write *S* if it tells about the kind of *step*. When you have completed the exercise, look back at the chart of the domain to see how well you did.

_____ 1. stroll   _____ 6. stumble

_____ 2. tiptoe   _____ 7. toddle

_____ 3. roam   _____ 8. ramble

_____ 4. hobble   _____ 9. wander

_____ 5. saunter   _____ 10. stagger

Part B

Repeat this exercise with the verbs below. Write *A* if the verb tells about the *attitude* of the person who is walking and *S* if it describes the *speed*.

_____ 1. edge   _____ 5. sneak

_____ 2. shuffle   _____ 6. inch

_____ 3. hurry   _____ 7. prowl

_____ 4. strut   _____ 8. swagger

Exercise 3: Sentence Completion

Choose the verb that best completes the sentence and then write it on the line.

A Neighborhood Fire

Yesterday a house on Stafford Street caught fire. A teenage boy across the street called the fire department the minute he saw the smoke. As soon as the fire trucks arrived, the firefighters jumped out and (1) (rambled/hurried) to the back of the truck to get the hoses. The fire chief quickly checked around the outside of the house and made sure no one was in the house. Then he (2) (hastened/shuffled) into the house with one of the fire hoses.

It was 5:30 P.M. and people were starting to come home from work. A crowd was gathering outside the house. A very young child was watching the fire and started to (3) (tiptoe/toddle) toward one of the firefighters. His mother quickly grabbed the child and picked him up. A reporter from the local paper arrived on the scene. There were so many people watching the fire that it wasn't easy for her to (4) (slouch/edge) her way through the crowd.

One of the firefighters injured his ankle when he fell from a ladder. He (5) (prowled/hobbled) back to the truck. He yelled in pain when he also (6) (stumbled/sauntered) over a child's bicycle that was lying on its side in the front yard. Another firefighter inhaled too much smoke while she was fighting the fire inside the house. She (7) (strutted/staggered) back to the truck and sat down next to the other injured firefighter.

The water from the hoses turned the grass to mud. It became more and more difficult for the firefighters to walk through it. They (8) (plodded/strolled) back and forth through the mud until the fire was out.

The next day, many people from the neighborhood (9) (waddled/wandered) by the wreckage of the house. Inside they could see the fire investigator who was (10) (inching/marching) carefully through each room of the house. He was trying to find the cause of the fire. The neighbors felt sorry for the family that had lost its home.

1. _____

2. _____

3. _____

4. _____

5. _____

6. _____

7. _____

8. _____

9. _____

10. _____

Exercise 4: Matching

Part A

Match each sentence with the WALK verb that best describes the situation. Write the verb on the line.

stumble   strut
hasten   trudge
march

1. Juan is walking in a parade.

1. _____

2. Diane is walking home. She is unhappy because she lost her wallet.

2. _____

3. Mr. Lee is walking to his office from the parking lot. He is late for an appointment.

3. _____

4. Eric walked into the kitchen to tell his mother he got an A on a test.

4. _____

5. Carmen hit her foot on a small rock as she was walking on a path.

5. _____

Part B

Now match these sentences with the WALK verb that best describes the situation. Write the verb on the line. For some situations there may be more than one correct answer.

edge	hobble
shuffle	slink
saunter	pace

1. Sue broke her leg and now has a cast on it.

1. _____

2. Keiko is trying to walk to the other side of a very crowded room.

2. _____

3. Tomas is walking home. He is tired and unhappy because he had a bad day at school.

3. _____

4. Helen is walking in the park. She is waiting for a friend who is 30 minutes late.

4. _____

5. Bill doesn't want anyone to notice him as he walks into the room.

5. _____

Exercise 5: Word Choice

The sentences below will help you see how the verbs in the WALK domain add extra meaning to sentences. Cross out the verb <u>walk</u> and replace it with a verb from the WALK domain that will make the sentence more expressive. More than one verb can be used in some sentences. Be ready to explain your choice.

Example: The opera singer ~~walked~~ ? off the stage while the audience continued applauding.

Ex. ____strutted____

1. Nick walked ? through the deep snow to feed the hungry animals in the barn.

1. _____

2. This morning Johannes overslept and was late for work. He didn't want the boss to know, so he walked ? past her office.

2. _____

3. Sometimes I like to walk ? through shopping malls just looking in the windows of the shops.

3. _____

4. The lawyer walked ? out of the courtroom after hearing the guilty verdict for his client.

4. _____

5. I broke my ankle while I was skiing last weekend. Tomorrow when I walk ? into class everyone will have a good laugh.

5. _____

6. I got sick at work yesterday. But I stayed in the office until I had finished my project. At 7:30 P.M. I walked ? into my house. I felt so bad that I went to bed right away.

6. _____

7. Rick was wearing his new suit. He walked _?_ into the living room to show everyone how handsome he looked.

7. _____

8. Tourists should spend some time walking _?_ around the cities they visit. This will help them understand what the city is really like.

8. _____

9. Kenji had been sick for three days. He got out of bed, walked _?_ a few steps and then fell down.

9. _____

10. Sometimes when I am so nervous that I can't sit still, I walk _?_ back and forth in my room.

10. _____

Exercise 6: For Discussion

Part A

Some verbs in the WALK domain, like hasten and hurry, tell us mainly about the speed at which someone is walking. The other verbs tell us about the manner of walking. The manner of walking verbs often tell us something about speed, too. For example, because wander means to walk without a goal, people often wander slowly. Because limp means to walk like someone with an injured foot, people usually limp slowly. (It is possible to limp quickly, but that is more unusual.)

In a small group or with your teacher, discuss the following WALK verbs. Does the verb usually describe fast walking or slow walking? Put the verb in the best place on the chart below. Wander and limp have been done for you.

plod	slouch	hasten	falter
amble	trudge	inch	strut
swagger	hurry	march	creep
stride	shuffle	stroll	sneak
tiptoe	prowl	limp	slink
edge	pace		

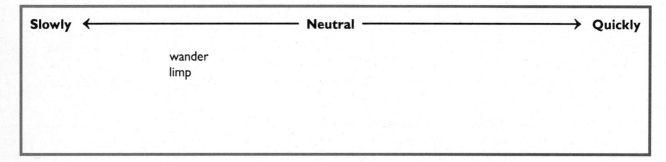

Part B

As you learned above, people usually limp slowly. But it is also possible to limp quickly. Can you think of a situation in which someone might limp quickly? For one or two of the other verbs on the chart, think of an unusual situation when someone might walk at a different speed than is shown by their placement on the chart.

Exercise 7: For Discussion or Writing

Imagine that it is a hot summer evening and you are sitting on the porch. You are watching people who are walking by. Make up five sentences that describe what you see. Use some of the following verbs from the WALK domain.

hobble   sneak   trudge   roam   falter
strut   ramble   pace   hasten

VI. Expanding the Domain

Figurative Meanings

Some of the verbs in the WALK domain can be used to refer to <u>talking</u> as well as to <u>walking</u>. What do you think the following sentences mean?

a. During the lecture the professor <u>rambled</u> on and on. I had no idea what she was trying to say.
b. The boy was so nervous that he <u>stumbled</u> over his words.
c. The politician <u>plodded</u> through his speech. When he finished, many people in the audience were asleep.

In these sentences, the verbs ramble, stumble, and <u>plod</u> don't tell about walking. They are describing ways of talking. For example, when the professor rambles on, she talks with no goal. When the boy stumbles over his words, he talks unsteadily. The verbs in the examples are not being used in their literal sense – their real, walk sense. They are being used figuratively. Words are often used this way in English.

Exercise 8: Literal or Figurative?

In the sentences below some of the underlined verbs are used figuratively and others are used literally. Write *F* if the verb is used *figuratively* and *L* if it is used *literally.*

Example: ___F___ The candidate <u>tiptoed</u> around the real issues of the election.

_____ 1. The hiker <u>wandered</u> from the trail and was lost in the mountains <u>for</u> two days.

_____ 2. Young people who <u>wander</u> from the teachings of their parents often regret their actions.

_____ 3. The professor <u>roamed</u> so far from his main idea that I had a hard time taking notes.

_____ 4. The lawyer confidently <u>strode</u> to the front of the courtroom.

_____ 5. The small hole in the carpet caught my heel and caused me to <u>falter</u> as I walked into the room.

_____ 6. The groom was so nervous during the wedding ceremony that he <u>faltered</u> as he said his vows.

_____ 7. No one was laughing at the comedian's jokes, but he <u>limped</u> his way through the rest of his routine anyway.

_____ 8. I don't like reading historical novels, but I had to <u>plod</u> through this book because it was an assignment for my English class.

_____ 9. The police officer told Mary about the fire. But he <u>hastened</u> to add that no one had been injured.

_____ 10. Is the world <u>edging</u> toward another world war?

Exercise 9: Reading

The paragraphs below are about learning vocabulary. As you read them, underline any verbs you find from the WALK domain. When you have finished reading, go back and put a circle around each verb that has been used figuratively.

Learning New Words

Students have different attitudes about learning new words. Some students don't like to learn new words. They sometimes sneak away when it's time to study vocabulary. They creep through their vocabulary lessons. They plod to the dictionary, thinking about all the words they don't know. They stumble from page to page, trying to find the word they are looking up.

5

Other students like to learn new words. They hurry to the dictionary, eager to find the meaning of a new word. They even enjoy roaming through the dictionary on their own. They look for interesting new words as they wander from page to page. They aren't upset by a vocabulary list. They enjoy preparing their vocabulary assignments.

10

Now that you have finished the first chapter of this book, what kind of attitude do you have? Do you like the idea of learning vocabulary through domains? Do you want to march right on to the next lesson? Will it be fun and interesting for you? You should be able to learn more words more quickly. Now you should be ready to stride with confidence through the rest of the

15

chapters in this book. Good luck!

Let's Talk

THE TALK DOMAIN

I. Getting Ready

The TALK Domain

Humans talk. In fact, it's our ability to talk that makes us different from animals. Some people like to talk more than others. They enjoy chatting with their friends or their family. Others are more silent. They only talk when they have something important to say or when someone talks to them. Discuss the following questions with your whole class or in a small group.

1. Do you know anyone who talks too much? Do you enjoy being with that person?

2. Do you know anyone who doesn't talk much? Do you enjoy being with that person?

3. How do you talk when children are sleeping in the next room and you don't want to wake them up?

4. How do you talk when you have a bad phone connection?

II. Introducing the Domain

Because talking is an important human activity, there are many verbs for talk in English. All the words in the TALK domain have the same basic meaning as talk. But each word has some additional meaning as well. Look over the domain below and mark the words that you don't know.

The TALK Domain

Soft
whisper
mumble
murmur
mutter
grumble

Loud
shout
scream
yell
holler
shriek
roar
bellow

Unimportant Talking
■ *Informal*

chat   blabber
chatter   jabber
chitchat rattle on
gab   bend someone's ear
yak   run off at the mouth
babble

III. Exploring the Domain

A. The movie theater is slowly filling with people who are anxious to see the hit movie of the summer, which will begin in about five minutes. The audience is munching popcorn or eating chocolate candy, and

talking. In the back row, two young girls are chitchatting about their plans for the weekend. They will probably chatter until the movie begins. In the row in front of them, two teenagers are rattling on about their chemistry teacher. It's obvious that they don't like the grades they just received! A young couple is chatting about the new car they just bought.

In another row, a middle-aged couple is waiting for the movie to begin. Only the wife, Andrea, is talking. She is bending her husband's ear about something that happened to her at work that day. Her husband, John, opens his mouth every once in a while as though he would like to add a word or two, but Andrea is babbling so fast that he doesn't have a chance! He wonders if she will ever stop yakking at him.

chat
chatter
chitchat
gab
yak
babble
blabber
jabber
rattle on
bend someone's ear
run off at the mouth

B. As the lights dim, the theater becomes quiet. But Andrea continues to talk. Now she is grumbling about her mother-in-law. She is muttering that her mother-in-law talks too much. Suddenly John stands up, mumbles something to Andrea about popcorn, and walks up the aisle.

A few other people continue to talk quietly. A mother is whispering to her son, reminding him that he has to sit still during the movie. He murmurs, "Yes, Mom," and then continues eating his popcorn.

whisper
mumble
murmur
mutter
grumble

C. The movie is an exciting drama. In one scene, the two main characters, a young couple, are having dinner in an expensive restaurant. Suddenly, they begin to shout and yell at each other. Just as the man at the next table hollers at them to be quiet, the husband stands up. He bellows at his wife that she's the most selfish woman he's ever met. She shrieks that she never wants to see him again. Then, as the husband stomps angrily out of

shout
scream
yell
holler
shriek
roar
bellow

the restaurant, he stops, turns back to his wife's table and roars, "And don't forget to leave a tip!" She screams that she always leaves bigger tips than he does, throws some money on the table, and leaves the restaurant.

D. When the movie is over, the people inch their way up the aisle and out of the theater. Some of them are gabbing about the movie and others are jabbering about where to go for pizza. Now Andrea is running off at the mouth about all the bad movies that are being shown. John is wondering if she will ever stop blabbering at him.

IV. Exercises

Exercise 1: Beginning Practice

Spend a few minutes studying the domain on page 12. Then without looking at the domain, put each of the words in its correct place in the chart given below. When you have finished, use the domain to check your answers.

holler	murmur	jabber
yell	shout	rattle on
chitchat	whisper	grumble
roar	shriek	bellow
mutter	mumble	chatter
chat	scream	babble
gab	yak	run off at the mouth

The TALK Domain

Soft   **Loud**

Unimportant Talking
■ *Informal*

Exercise 2: More Practice

Add a word in each group that is similar in meaning.

1. babble, rattle on, chatter

2. holler, roar, shout

3. mutter, mumble, whisper

4. chitchat, bend someone's ear, gab

5. bellow, shriek, scream

6. grumble, murmur, whisper

1. _____

2. _____

3. _____

4. _____

5. _____

6. _____

Exercise 3: Matching

Match the sentence with the TALK verb that best describes the situation. Write the verb on the line.

holler   chat
murmur   grumble
run off at the mouth   yell

1. Two women are talking over the fence in the backyard.

2. The lights are out and the house is quiet, but two children are telling secrets to each other in bed.

3. A mother's child is across the street and she wants him to come home for dinner.

4. Two factory workers are sitting in the cafeteria during their lunch hour. They are complaining about the bad working conditions.

5. A father is angry because his son came home very late.

6. A man talks for half an hour at a meeting about a topic that is of interest only to him.

1. _____

2. _____

3. _____

4. _____

5. _____

6. _____

Exercise 4: Sentence Completion

The following conversation began in the library of an American university. Choose the word that best completes the sentence and write it on the line.

gabbing   yelled   murmured   shouted   whispered

"Dave, I'm done with my calculus, so I'm going to the Student Union for a break. Do you want to come?" Kirsten (1) .

1. _____

"I'll meet you there in a few minutes. I want to finish this problem first," Dave (2) .

2. _____

"OK. See you in a few minutes."

Kirsten was strolling to the Student Union when she saw her friend Alan on the other side of the street.

"Hey, Alan," she (3) . "Come on over to the Union. Dave and I are going to have some pizza."

3. _____

"Sorry, Kirsten," Alan (4) back. "I've got to finish a computer program. It's due today."

4. _____

Half an hour later Dave had joined Kirsten in the Student Union and soon they were (5) about their plans for the weekend.

5. _____

Exercise 5: Sense or Nonsense?

When a situation makes sense, it is usual, reasonable, expected, or appropriate. For example, in an expensive, elegant restaurant, it is usual for people to whisper or chatter quietly.

When a situation doesn't make sense, it is silly, illogical, unexpected, or inappropriate. For example, it doesn't make sense to bellow in an expensive restaurant. It is an inappropriate way to act. The opposite of making sense is nonsense.

Part A

Decide whether each of the sentences below makes sense or is nonsense. Then circle the correct word.

1. Mona and Eric are on a camping trip. Suddenly Mona sees a huge snake. She shrieks, "Help, Eric!"   SENSE   NONSENSE

2. Bertrand is being interviewed for a new job. He blabbers for twenty minutes about his last job.   SENSE   NONSENSE

3. Julia is a singer and she is on TV for the first time. She is on a talk show telling about her new album. She mutters her answers to all the questions.   SENSE   NONSENSE

4. Sally is at a picnic with some friends. She sees Ana in the parking lot and hollers, "We're over here, Ana."   SENSE   NONSENSE

5. During a performance of Beethoven's Fifth Symphony at the Lincoln Center in New York, Ron grumbles to his wife that he doesn't like the music.   SENSE   NONSENSE

Part B

Write four TALK sentences of your own that either make sense or are nonsense. Be ready to share your sentences with your classmates.

Exercise 6: For Writing

Individually or with a partner, write a dialogue similar to the one in Exercise 4. Your dialogue might take place:

1. at a baseball game,
2. during a break between classes,
3. in a doctor's waiting room,

or any place that is interesting to you. Try to have the people in your dialogue talk in as many different ways as possible. Use as many words from the TALK domain as you can. If you are not sure how to punctuate a dialogue, ask your teacher for help.

V. Expanding the Domain

Animal Sounds

Sometimes verbs that express the sound an animal makes are used to mean talk. You might read a paragraph like this in a newspaper or magazine.

The face of the 13-year-old drug dealer was covered with tears. "Stop crying," the police officer barked at the young boy. "Drug dealers aren't supposed to cry!"

The word bark is usually used to indicate the loud noise that a dog makes. Why do you think the author used the word barked in the paragraph above? How was the officer talking?

Other animal sounds that can be used to mean talk are given in the chart below.

Animal Sounds	
Animal	**Sound**
dog	bark, howl, growl, snarl
cat	purr
bird	twitter, chirp
dove	coo
snake	hiss
pig	squeal, grunt

Exercise 7: For Discussion

Work in a small group. Read the sentences below and then discuss how you think the person is talking. Use your knowledge of the animals in the chart to help you.

1. The sergeant snarled his orders to the new soldiers.

2. Stacey squealed when the rock star appeared on the stage.

3. The actress purred her answer to the reporters.

4. The prisoner grunted his reply to the guard.

5. My grandmother is so cute when she twitters about her grandchildren.

Exercise 8: For Discussion

Read the following sentences.

1. Don't tell him any secrets. He's a real blabbermouth.
2. Katie is a chatterbox. She loves to talk.

You already know what blabber and chatter mean. What kind of a person do you think a blabbermouth or a chatterbox is? How would you feel if someone called you a blabbermouth or a chatterbox?

UNIT 3

The Tortoise and the Hare

THE SPEED DOMAIN

I. Getting Ready

> ## The SPEED Domain

The tortoise (turtle) is an animal that moves very slowly. The hare (rabbit), on the other hand, usually runs very quickly. In many countries the turtle is a symbol for slow movement and the rabbit is a symbol for fast movement. Is this true in your country? Discuss the following questions with your whole class or in a small group.

1. How would you say these sentences in your language?

   The turtle moved slowly. The rabbit moved quickly.

2. What do you think this sentence means?

   He lost his job because he worked at a snail's pace.

II. Introducing the Domain

The pace or speed of life in our modern world is often quite fast. Fast food restaurants, FAX machines, and jet planes are all signs of the fast pace of life today. But life was not always lived at high speed. Our grandparents and great-grandparents lived at a much slower pace.

There are many words and expressions in English that tell whether an action is being done slowly or quickly. Look over the domain below and mark the words that you don't know.

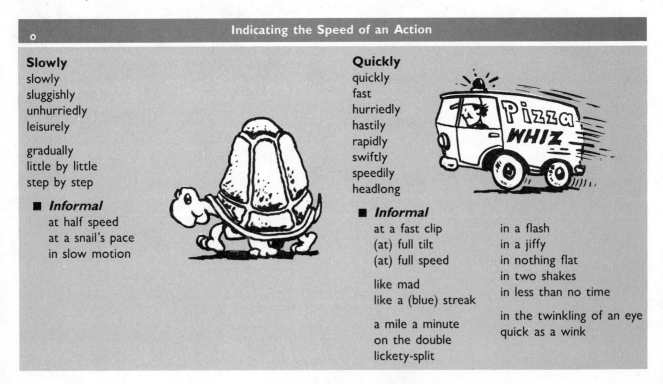

Indicating the Speed of an Action

Slowly
slowly
sluggishly
unhurriedly
leisurely

gradually
little by little
step by step

■ *Informal*
  at half speed
  at a snail's pace
  in slow motion

Quickly
quickly
fast
hurriedly
hastily
rapidly
swiftly
speedily
headlong

■ *Informal*
  at a fast clip
  (at) full tilt
  (at) full speed

  like mad
  like a (blue) streak

  a mile a minute
  on the double
  lickety-split

  in a flash
  in a jiffy
  in nothing flat
  in two shakes
  in less than no time

  in the twinkling of an eye
  quick as a wink

As you looked over this domain, did you notice that the informal expressions for <u>quickly</u> greatly outnumber those for <u>slowly</u>? Does this tell you anything about the people who speak this language?

III. Exploring the Domain

A. The American historian Will Durant said, "No man in a hurry is quite civilized." If he were alive today, Mr. Durant would probably find very few civilized Americans. Most of them seem to be in a hurry most of the time. They go <u>hurriedly</u> from store to store, rarely walking <u>leisurely</u> down the street. Clerks in grocery stores are expected to work <u>speedily</u>. In fact, those who work <u>at half speed</u> might lose their jobs. Americans seldom eat lunch <u>unhurriedly</u>. They <u>rapidly</u> gulp down a fast food lunch before returning to work.

In a survey taken in 1990, Americans were asked why they eat at fast food restaurants. Only 6 percent said it was because they liked the food. But 44 percent said they eat fast food because it's fast. They like being able to buy and eat their food <u>quickly</u>. Speed is definitely a part of American culture.

In other cultures, the pace of life is quite different. In France meals are generally eaten <u>slowly</u>, with great enjoyment. The French also like to wander <u>unhurriedly</u> along the street after enjoying a good meal in a nice restaurant.

Sometimes there are problems when someone from a fast-paced country meets someone from a country with a slower pace of life. One wants to do things <u>at full speed</u> and the other wants to do things more <u>gradually</u>. They might have a hard time understanding each other's idea of fast and slow.

B. How about you? Do you live your life at a slow or a fast pace? Are you an early bird who wakes up at dawn and then jumps <u>headlong</u> into the day's activities? Or are you more of a night owl who wakes up <u>little by little</u> and then moves <u>sluggishly</u> through the morning hours?

How will you do the exercises that follow this paragraph? Will you do them <u>in a jiffy</u> or <u>at a snail's pace</u>?

IV. Exercises

Exercise 1: Beginning Practice

Study the SPEED domain for a few minutes. Then, without looking at it, write *S* (*slow* speed) or *F* (*fast* speed) on the lines below. When you have completed the exercise, look back at the domain to see how well you did.

_____ **1.** swiftly   _____ **4.** like mad

_____ **2.** in a flash   _____ **5.** gradually

_____ **3.** unhurriedly   _____ **6.** lickety-split

_____ 7. in two shakes

_____ 8. little by little

_____ 9. on the double

_____ 10. in slow motion

_____ 11. quick as a wink

_____ 12. at full tilt

_____ 13. hastily

_____ 14. at half speed

_____ 15. in less than no time

_____ 16. step by step

_____ 17. rapidly

_____ 18. like a blue streak

_____ 19. hurriedly

_____ 20. in nothing flat

Exercise 2: More Practice

Cross out the word or expression that doesn't belong.

1. at half speed   step by step   like mad   in slow motion

2. rapidly   sluggishly   hastily   speedily

3. in the twinkling of an eye   gradually   unhurriedly   slowly

4. at a fast clip   at half speed   in a flash   in two shakes

5. quick as a wink   swiftly   hastily   little by little

Exercise 3: Word Puzzles

Part A

Write words or phrases from the SPEED domain that mean slowly or quickly.
When you finish, the letters in the boxes will spell the name of an animal that
moves swiftly.

a   _   f   _   _   t   □   l   _   p

_   n   o   t   □   _   n   _   l   _   t

_   p   e   □   _   i   _   _

_   h   □   _   _   l   _   _   g

h   _   s   □   _   _   y

_   □   _   p   _   d   _   y

i   _   t   o   _   □   a   _   e   _

The fastest animal in the world is the _____ .

Part B

Now write words from the SPEED domain that mean SLOWLY. When you finish, the letters in the boxes will spell the name of an animal that moves slowly.

i   _   s   l   _   w   _   o   □   _   o   n

_   r   _   d   □   _   l   _   _

_   n   _   u   r   □   _   _   d   _   _

_   t   _   p   _   y   _   □   _   p

a   _   s   a   _   □   's p   _   _   e

_   e   _   s   _   r   □   _   _

A _____ usually moves slowly.

Exercise 4: Sentence Completion

Choose the appropriate word or expression to complete the sentence. Then write it on the line.

Example: If no one interrupts me, I'll finish my homework ___?___ .
(*in a flash, at a snail's pace*)

Ex. _____ in a flash _____

1. My friend John is a full-time student and has a part-time job. He always eats his lunch ___?___ . (*on the double, in slow motion*)

   1. _____

2. At the shopping mall, the young couple sauntered ___?___ from store to store. (*leisurely, hastily*)

   2. _____

3. Tom and Eric work for the same company. Tom was promoted because he always did his work ___?___ . Eric wasn't promoted. His supervisor said he worked too slowly. (*quickly, leisurely*)

   3. _____

4. It was 6:30 P.M. Javier wanted to see a movie that started at 7:30, but he had to finish his homework. So he worked ___?___ for fifteen minutes and made it to the movie on time. (*sluggishly, like mad*)

   4. _____

5. There was an accident and a child was near death. The doctor worked ___?___ to stop the bleeding. (*unhurriedly, swiftly*)

   5. _____

6. The dog ran out the door ___?___ and chased the squirrel up the tree. (*at full tilt, at half speed*)

   6. _____

7. ___?___ students learn how to write an essay in English. (*Step by step, In the twinkling of an eye*)

   7. _____

8. Sarah typed ___?___ because it was already 4:50 P.M. and her report was due at 5:00 P.M. (*speedily, little by little*)

   8. _____

9. Joe just bought himself a microwave oven and now he can cook dinner ___?___ . (*at a snail's pace, in a jiffy*)

   9. _____

10. Joe's grandmother thinks microwave ovens make food taste bad. She still prepares her meals ___?___ over several hours. (*gradually, hastily*)

    10. _____

11. People used to think that the best way to get somewhere ___?___ was by riding a horse. (*rapidly, sluggishly*)

    11. _____

12. Today the horse seems very slow compared to a modern car that can go a distance of fifty miles ___?___ . (*in less than no time, at half speed*)

    12. _____

13. Before the invention of the printing press, people made copies of documents and books ___?___ , using paper and pen. (*slowly, quickly*)

    13. _____

14. Today, a photocopy machine can make a copy ___?___ . (*in nothing flat, little by little*)

    14. _____

Exercise 5: Sense or Nonsense?

Decide whether each of the sentences below makes sense or is nonsense. Then circle the correct word.

1. The teacher was late! He hurried sluggishly to his classroom.	SENSE	NONSENSE
2. She jabbered a mile a minute for a whole hour.	SENSE	NONSENSE
3. He inched his way rapidly toward the dark house.	SENSE	NONSENSE
4. They ambled unhurriedly around the plaza.	SENSE	NONSENSE
5. The old man shuffled at full tilt into the kitchen.	SENSE	NONSENSE
6. The wounded police officer staggered hastily to his car.	SENSE	NONSENSE
7. Little by little the coffee dripped into the pot.	SENSE	NONSENSE
8. After Tim fell and hit his head, his mother drove him to the hospital at half speed.	SENSE	NONSENSE
9. A FAX arrives at its destination in less than no time.	SENSE	NONSENSE
10. The service in that restaurant is great. The waiter brought my order quick as a wink.	SENSE	NONSENSE

Exercise 6: Reading

Part A

"The Tortoise and the Hare" is a well-known story written by Aesop, a Greek storyteller. Each of his stories has a moral, a lesson to be learned. Read the story and then do the exercises that follow.

The Tortoise and the Hare

by Aesop

The Hare was talking to the other animals about how fast he could run. "I'm the fastest runner among you! I have never lost a race!" He looked around at the other animals. "Who would like to race with me?"

The Tortoise quietly said, "I would."

"Ha! That's a good joke," said the Hare. "I could dance circles around you 5 all the way."

"I wouldn't say that until you've actually won," answered the Tortoise. "Let's go. Let's see who is the fastest."

So the other animals decided where the Tortoise and the Hare should run and the race began. The Hare ran quickly and was soon out of sight. 10

It was a scorching hot day and the Hare soon became tired. He knew he was far ahead of the Tortoise. He decided that he had plenty of time to lie down under a tree and rest. Within a few minutes, he was fast asleep.

The Tortoise never stopped. He plodded on and on. When the Hare finally woke up from his nap, he quickly leaped up and looked around. He was 15 horrified to see that the Tortoise was about to cross the finish line. The Hare knew that it would be impossible for him to catch up to the Tortoise.

The Tortoise smiled as he looked back at the Hare. "You see," he said. "Slow and steady wins the race."

Part B

Do the following activities.

1. Discuss what you think the moral (the lesson) of this tale is.

2. Retell the story using as many words and expressions from the domain as you can. Keep the formal tone of the story.

3. Retell the story using an informal tone. Imagine that you are telling it to a young child. You will need to use different words and expressions from the domain this time.

Exercise 7: For Discussion

The lesson or moral of the story of the tortoise and the hare is that slow, steady work is often better than fast, careless work. Another way to say this in English is: *Haste makes waste.*

1. Can you think of some activities that should be done slowly and carefully? What activities should be done quickly?

2. Do you have a similar expression in your native language?

Exercise 8: For Discussion or Writing

Discuss and/or write about the pace of life in your native country. Try to give examples of some activities that people do at a fast pace or at a slow pace.

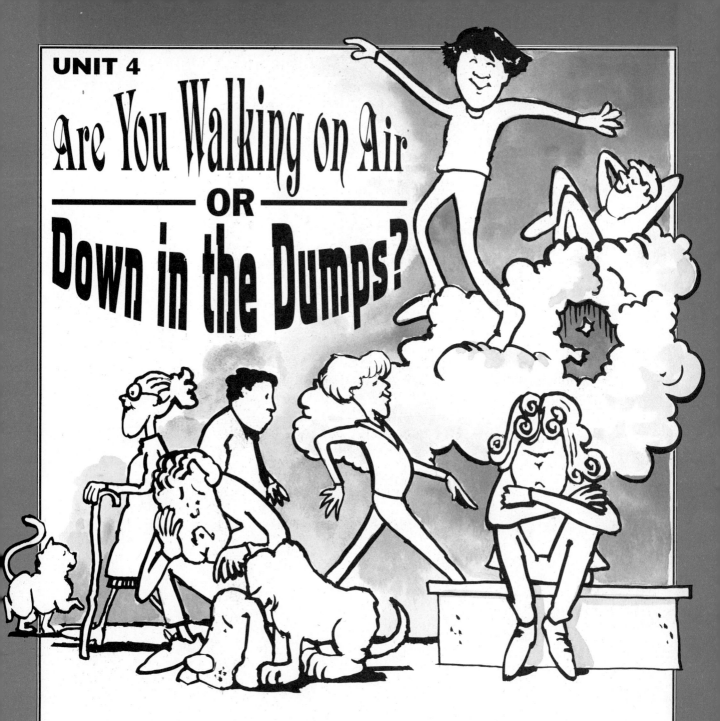

Are You Walking on Air
OR
Down in the Dumps?

THE HAPPY—SAD DOMAIN

I. Getting Ready

The HAPPY—SAD Domain

Have you ever watched a movie or a television program in a language you didn't understand? Could you tell whether the characters were feeling happy or sad even though you didn't know what they were saying? You probably could because people communicate their feelings through body language, or non-verbal communication, as well as through words. One common sign of happiness is a smile. Discuss the following questions with your whole class or in a small group.

1. Can you think of other facial expressions or movements that people in your country use to show that they feel happy?
2. What do people do with their eyebrows, shoulders, or hands when they feel sad?

II. Introducing the Domain

Although we often use non-verbal communication to express our emotions, we also use words. The domain below gives adjectives that are used to describe emotions from very happy to very sad. Look over the domain and mark the words that you don't know.

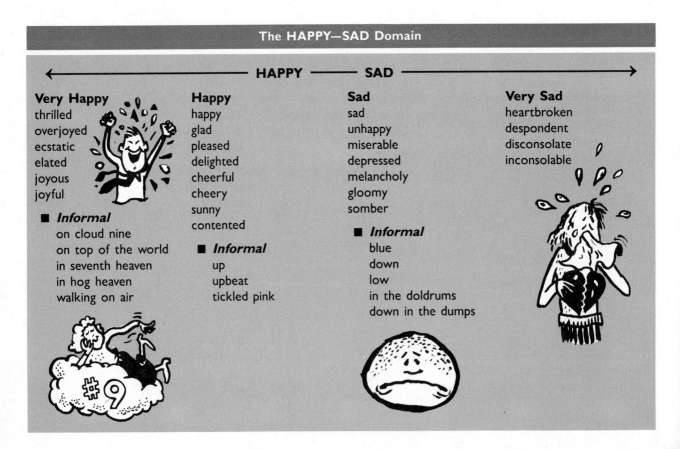

The HAPPY—SAD Domain

←————— HAPPY ——— SAD —————→

Very Happy
thrilled
overjoyed
ecstatic
elated
joyous
joyful

■ *Informal*
on cloud nine
on top of the world
in seventh heaven
in hog heaven
walking on air

Happy
happy
glad
pleased
delighted
cheerful
cheery
sunny
contented

■ *Informal*
up
upbeat
tickled pink

Sad
sad
unhappy
miserable
depressed
melancholy
gloomy
somber

■ *Informal*
blue
down
low
in the doldrums
down in the dumps

Very Sad
heartbroken
despondent
disconsolate
inconsolable

III. Exploring the Domain

A. In the United States, if you turn on the TV in the early afternoon, you will probably tune in to a soap opera. These daily programs tell the story of several main characters. Many viewers become "addicted" to a soap opera because they get to know the characters on the program very well. The characters become like friends and the viewers want to know what will happen to them next.

The characters in soap operas live interesting lives. In fact, there is seldom a dull moment! Deaths, births, marriages, murders, fights, divorces—it all happens in a soap opera.

B. Let's tune in to a typical soap opera. On Monday's show, Sandra and Nick seem <u>pleased</u> and <u>contented</u> with their lives. Sandra is <u>delighted</u> with her new baby, and her husband, Nick, seems to be in a <u>cheery</u> mood, too. They are <u>glad</u> to be parents. Their baby has a <u>sunny</u>, <u>cheerful</u> disposition and everything is going well.

happy	cheerful
glad	cheery
pleased	sunny
delighted	contented

C. On the other hand, Sandra's mother, Emma, is <u>miserable</u>. She has been <u>depressed</u> ever since she became a grandmother. She thinks she is too young to be a grandmother. She becomes <u>gloomy</u> whenever she thinks about growing old. She is afraid she will lose her beauty. Sandra's sister, Elaine, is also feeling <u>unhappy</u>. She has become quite <u>melancholy</u> since the birth of Sandra's baby. No one in the family knows why she has become so <u>somber</u> lately.

sad	melancholy
unhappy	gloomy
miserable	somber
depressed	

D. This quiet life never lasts long in a soap opera! On Tuesday, the new baby is kidnapped. Sandra and Nick are <u>inconsolable</u> and Emma and Elaine are <u>heartbroken</u>. The baby's nanny feels responsible for the disaster because the baby was kidnapped while she was taking care of her. She is so <u>disconsolate</u> that her doctor gives her a tranquilizer. The police haven't received any ransom requests and have found no clues, so they have little hope of finding the child. Sandra becomes so <u>despondent</u> that Nick is afraid she might have a nervous breakdown.

heartbroken
despondent
disconsolate
inconsolable

E. In the world of soap operas, events happen quickly. By Friday the baby has been found. Sandra is <u>overjoyed</u> to have her baby back and Nick is <u>ecstatic</u>. Even Emma seems to be able to forget that she's a grandmother long enough to celebrate the <u>joyous</u> occasion. At first the nanny is <u>elated</u> by the return of the child. Later she announces that she is going to leave the family because of all the bad memories she has of the kidnapping. Even this announcement can't stop everyone from sharing a <u>joyful</u> meal. They are all <u>thrilled</u> with the happy ending to the story.

> thrilled
> overjoyed
> ecstatic
> elated
> joyous
> joyful

Tune in next Monday to see what happens in the exciting lives of Sandra, Nick, Emma, and Elaine!

F. *Informal Words and Expressions.* Look back at the informal words and expressions in the HAPPY–SAD domain on page 28. What direction is associated with happiness? How about sadness? What colors are associated with happiness and sadness? In your language do you use color or direction to indicate happiness or sadness?

The expression <u>in the doldrums</u> is a sailing term. A sailing ship is <u>in the doldrums</u> when it can't move because there is no wind. How do you think the sailors feel when that happens?

IV. Exercises

Exercise 1: Beginning Practice

Cross out the word or expression that doesn't belong.

1. depressed   somber   gloomy   sunny

2. melancholy   ecstatic   miserable   unhappy

3. contented   cheerful   disconsolate   delighted

4. happy as a clam   upbeat   pleased   inconsolable

5. down in the dumps   in hog heaven   cheery   on top of the world

Exercise 2: Word Choice

Cross out the word happy or sad in each sentence below. Choose a word or expression from the HAPPY–SAD domain that will make the sentence more expressive.

Example: Rainy days make me feel ~~sad~~ __?__ .

Ex. _____gloomy_____

1. I was ~~happy~~ __?__ when I got an A in English.

1. _____

2. I can see by your smile that you are ~~happy~~ __?__ .

2. _____

3. I just won $100,000 in the lottery! I am very ~~happy~~ __?__ !

3. _____

4. Peter was feeling a little ~~sad~~ __?__ yesterday, so his friends tried to cheer him up.

4. _____

5. I always feel ~~sad~~ __?__ when I have an argument with a friend.

5. _____

6. We're going to get married! I'm very ~~happy~~ __?__ .

6. _____

7. If I got fired from my job I would be ~~sad~~ __?__ .

7. _____

8. Harry was very ~~sad~~ __?__ when he learned of the death of his sister.

8. _____

9. Anne was ~~happy~~ __?__ when she got first place in the 10K race.

9. _____

10. I feel ~~sad~~ __?__ for several hours after I watch a really depressing movie.

10. _____

Exercise 3: Analogies

Look at the example of an analogy given below.

Example: Hot is to cold as up is to *down*.

The first two underlined words are related: hot is the opposite of cold. This analogy is completed by finding a word that is related to up in the same way that hot is related to cold. Since down is the opposite of up, it completes the analogy.

Analogies are not always sets of opposites. In the example below, the underlined words are synonyms.

Example: Very happy is to thrilled as very sad is to __?__ .

Ex. _____heartbroken_____

Complete the analogies below with a word from the HAPPY–SAD domain.

1. Melancholy is to depressed as elated is to __?__ .

1. _____

2. Thrilled is to joyful as heartbroken is to __?__ .

2. _____

3. Happy is to overjoyed as sad is to __?__ .

3. _____

4. Happy as a lark is to blue as upbeat is to __?__ .

4. _____

5. In the doldrums is to somber as on cloud nine is to __?__ .

5. _____

Exercise 4: Sense or Nonsense?

Decide whether each of the sentences makes sense or is nonsense. Then circle the correct word.

1. He's very cheery these days because he lost his job.	SENSE	NONSENSE
2. She was tickled pink by her best friend's invitation to spend a week at the ocean.	SENSE	NONSENSE
3. A person who is often melancholy would be a good teacher.	SENSE	NONSENSE
4. It is not appropriate to play joyous music at a funeral.	SENSE	NONSENSE
5. Some people are in seventh heaven when they are eating a chocolate sundae.	SENSE	NONSENSE
6. Carol was ecstatic last week because her boyfriend never called her.	SENSE	NONSENSE

Exercise 5: Reading and Writing

Ms. Appleton is an advice columnist. People write letters to her and tell her their problems. In her newspaper column, she gives advice on how to solve the problems. Read this letter to Ms. Appleton from "Worried in Arizona." Then write a letter with your advice to "Worried." Tell him what he should do to help his friend.

Dear Ms. Appleton,

I have been miserable lately because of my best friend. He used to be a happy person who liked to laugh and have fun. He had a really cheery personality. But lately he has become despondent and he's always too depressed to go out with us. I don't know what to do. He doesn't seem to enjoy life anymore and now his grades in school are going down. His parents got a divorce last year so now he only sees his father on weekends. Do you think he's so gloomy because of his parents' divorce? How can I help him get back to his old sunny self?

Worried in Arizona

Start your letter like this:

Dear Worried,

Exercise 6: For Writing

Look at the pictures below. Then write five or six sentences that tell the story of what happened in the pictures. In your story, use as many words from the HAPPY–SAD domain as possible.

Exercise 7: For Writing and Discussion

Write down short descriptions of four events in your life that made you feel happy or sad. Choose one event that made you feel *very happy*, one that made you feel *happy*, one that made you feel *sad*, and one that made you feel *very sad*. In your description, do not tell how you felt. You should only describe the event or situation.

In a small group, read your descriptions out loud. Your partners should then choose words from the HAPPY–SAD domain that they think describe how each event made you feel. Discuss with your partners the word that *you* would choose to describe your feelings.

V. Expanding the Domain

A. The words below show the idea that the heart is the center of human emotions. Which of the words below do you think means happy? Which mean sad? Do you have expressions like this in your language?

     light-hearted   heavy-hearted   broken-hearted

B. We often use the words <u>spirit</u> and <u>mood</u> to talk about happiness and sadness, as in the expressions below. Which of these expressions do you think mean happy? Which means sad? Do you have a word or words in your language that are similar to <u>spirit</u> or <u>mood</u>?

in good spirits   in a good mood   in a bad mood

C. Clams are animals with shells that live in the ocean. Larks are a kind of bird. Are these two animals happier than most other animals? Probably not. But we use the informal expressions below to express happiness. Do you have similar expressions in your language?

happy as a clam   happy as a lark

D. Look up the noun <u>sorrow</u> and the verb <u>mourn</u> in your dictionary. Knowing the meanings of these words will help you understand the special kind of sadness expressed by the adjectives below.

sorrowful   mournful

Exercise 8: Word Choice

Part A

Choose one of the words or expressions from "Expanding the Domain" to describe each of these people.

1. A man who just lost his job is _____ .

2. A college student on summer vacation is _____ .

3. A woman whose car was just stolen is _____ .

4. An athlete who just lost the chance to compete in the Olympics is

_____ .

5. A young woman who is on the beach, listening to her favorite music

is _____ .

6. A person whose mother just died is _____ .

Part B

Now write four situations of your own that are similar to those in Part A. In a small group or with the whole class, read your situations out loud. Your classmates should choose words from "Expanding the Domain" to describe how the person in each situation feels.

Laugh and the World Laughs With You Cry and You Cry Alone

THE SMILE—LAUGH DOMAIN
THE CRY DOMAIN

In this unit we will look at two different domains. In the first sections, we will learn words in the SMILE—LAUGH domain. In later sections we will explore the CRY domain.

I. Getting Ready

What makes you smile or laugh? Discuss the following questions with your whole class or in a small group.

1. What movie or TV characters make you smile? What is it about them that makes you smile?
2. What recent movie or TV show made you laugh out loud? What happened that was so funny?
3. Who is your favorite comedian? Why do you like this comedian?

II. Introducing the Domain

The SMILE—LAUGH Domain

Listen to your teacher read this passage adapted from Milan Kundera's novel *The Book of Laughter and Forgetting*. Then discuss the questions with your class.

"Laughter? Does anyone ever care about laughter? I mean real laughter—beyond joking. Laughter as delight, free and easy, delight of delights.

I smiled at my sister and said come let's play laughter together. We quietly stretched out side by side on the bed and started laughing. At first, we just pretended, of course. Forced laughs. Ridiculous laughs. Laughs so silly they made us laugh. Then it came—real laughter. Bursting laughter, magnificent laughter, full and wild. . . And we laughed to the infinity of our laughter. . .O laughter! Laughter of delight, delight of laughter. Laughing deeply is living deeply."

1. What did one of the sisters do first? (a) smile (b) laugh quietly (c) laugh out loud
2. What did the sisters do last? (a) smile (b) laugh quietly (c) laugh out loud

The verbs in the SMILE and LAUGH domain can be divided into three groups according to the amount of sound that is made. There is one group for no sound, one for laughing quietly, and one for laughing loudly.

Look over the domain below and mark any words that you don't know.

The SMILE—LAUGH Domain

Smile
smile
grin
smirk

Laugh Quietly
giggle
chuckle
chortle
titter
snicker

Laugh Loudly
laugh out loud
burst out laughing
cackle
roar with laughter
howl with laughter
shriek with laughter

it wasn't long before the room was filled with laughter. The students really __(3)__ when a few of the boys and girls made paper airplanes and sent them flying across the room.

Fifteen minutes later, when the teacher came back into the room, the whole class was __(4)__ . The teacher yelled, "Stop it! Stop it right now!" The class suddenly got quiet, but most of the students couldn't help __(5)__ a little bit. The teacher said that he was going to make the whole class stay 15 minutes after school because of all the noise. There wasn't a sound in the room. Nobody felt like __(6)__ about this bad news.

3. _____

4. _____

5. _____

6. _____

Part B

After you have finished this exercise, go back and read the whole passage out loud.

Exercise 4: For Discussion or Writing

The atmosphere in American classrooms is relaxed. In some classes, you can hear students talking and laughing. Most of the time, this is not bad or inappropriate behavior. However, if a teacher leaves the room, the students should not be too noisy.

Discuss or write about this question: What do you think elementary school students in your country would do if the teacher was gone?

Exercise 5: Rhyming Words

Complete the following funny poems by adding a word from the SMILE–LAUGH domain that rhymes with or sounds the same as the underlined word.

Example: If you saw a giraffe kiss a calf,
    It would probably make you __?__ .

Ex. ___laugh___

1. There once was a lady named Wyn,
Who was always so terribly grim.
She'd never smile,
Though once in a while
You could almost see her __?__ .

1. _____

2. When they hear a good joke,
Some people scowl.
But I prefer people
Who know how to __?__ .

2. _____

3. If you saw a fat, green clown,
With a pink velvet buckle,
You might burst out laughing
Or maybe just __?__ .

3. _____

4. That movie was so funny,
For the rest of the week,
When we mentioned its name,
We did nothing but __?__ .

4. _____

5. Lazy Mary hated school,
　　She never did her work.
　　When the teacher bawled her out,
　　She'd just sit and   ?   .

5. _____

6. The turtle was slow and
　　The rabbit much quicker.
　　The turtle won,
　　So the rabbit can't   ?   .

6. _____

Exercise 6: Reading

Part A

Skim the following passage, underlining any words from the SMILE–LAUGH domain.

Don't worry if this reading seems difficult to you. You don't have to understand every sentence.

Researchers Find Laughter To Be A Powerful Medicine

What do you enjoy doing? Do you like strolling in the moonlight or do you prefer giggling over a funny scene in a movie?

　　An increasing number of scientists have found that anything that gives you pleasure may be more than just fun. Pleasure and humor might help us live longer, fight off illness, and cure drug addiction. "Science has generally neglected 5 pleasure and humor to concentrate on negative things like depression and illness," said Dr. William Fry, a psychiatry professor at Stanford University Medical Center in California. "But there's a growing realization of just how powerful pleasure is."

　　For example, research shows that smiling and laughing can actually strengthen your immune system, reduce stress and physical pain, and even help 10 cancer patients. One research project at Loma Linda University showed these beneficial effects of laughter on the body. In the study, ten medical students were hooked up to several machines and spent an hour watching a funny videotape of a man smashing watermelons with a hammer.

　　Researchers were not trying to prove that smashing watermelons is a funny 15 thing to do. They already knew that the volunteers would probably howl with laughter. What the researchers wanted to find out was how grinning, chuckling, and howling affected the volunteers as they watched the video.

　　The researchers were delighted to discover that small but important changes were taking place in the volunteers' bloodstreams as they giggled or roared with 20 laughter. Their blood showed increased production of white blood cells (the blood cells that defend us against infection and disease). At the same time, a decrease was noticed in the levels of chemicals that stop the immune system from working properly.

　　Studies such as this seem to show that you should laugh, chortle, and howl 25 as much as possible! You will increase your chances of living a long, healthy life. That's what one researcher means when he says, "He who laughs, lasts. For years we've thought that laughter and other forms of pleasure were good for you. Now it's a physiological reality."

Part B

Read the passage again carefully to find the answers to these questions.

1. What are the positive physical effects of grinning and laughing? List as many as you can.
2. In the study mentioned in the article, how did researchers learn that laughing was good for us?

Exercise 7: For Discusssion or Writing

Everybody in the whole world laughs, but different people laugh at different things. What do you think about these comedians: Charlie Chaplin, Bill Cosby, and Eddie Murphy? Some Americans might think they are really funny while other Americans might think they are not funny at all. Different kinds of humor make us laugh.

Discuss and/or write your answers to these questions.

1. What are some situations in which people in your country giggle? Are there any special gestures or body language that go with giggling?

---

2. In what situations do people in your country roar with laughter?
3. Have you noticed anything interesting about how Americans laugh? What kinds of things do Americans laugh about?
4. In English, we write "ha, ha!" to show laughter in a book or a cartoon. We write "tee, hee, hee" to show giggling. How do you write the general word for the sound of laughter in your culture? What is the written word to show the sound of giggling?

IV. Getting Ready

The CRY Domain

Now that you've had a good laugh, let's get ready for a good cry. Take a few minutes to answer the questions below. Discuss them with your whole class or in a small group.

1. You probably already know the meaning of the verb cry as it is used in this sentence:

    People often cry when they are sad.

    What word or words in your language mean cry?
2. Do people cry in different ways? Can you describe some of these different ways?
3. Do people always make noise when they cry?

V. Creating the CRY Domain

In English there are many verbs that have the same basic meaning as cry, such as weep, shed tears, and wail. Most of these verbs add some extra meaning to the concept of CRY. For example, wail means to cry loudly, usually with a great deal of emotion. The verbs sob and weep, like cry, are neutral in meaning. A person can sob quietly or loudly.

The following sentences will help you understand the meaning of the words in the CRY domain. After reading each sentence, see if you can create a chart for the CRY domain using the outline which follows. Add each underlined word or expression to the outline. Cry and wail have been done for you.

1. The little girl wailed when she heard that her pet kitten had been run over.

2. Psychologists say that people weep to deal with their feelings of sadness.

3. Sometimes our son Mark whimpers at night while he's sleeping. It's a very quiet kind of crying that doesn't last too long. Maybe he's having a bad dream. He never wakes up and he usually stops whimpering in a few seconds.

4. The little boy was very sad when his new electric train broke. He cried his eyes out for several days. He knew his parents couldn't afford to fix it or buy him a new one.

5. *John:* Do you want to go see the movie "Lost Loves" tonight?

   Kara: No, I don't think so. I read the movie review in the paper. It sounds like a real tear-jerker. I hate movies like that! Everybody starts bawling in the middle, and then you can hardly hear the movie!

   John: Oh, come on. It won't be that bad!

   Kara: No, no, no. You don't understand. I just can't stand it when people start blubbering like idiots and wiping their eyes just because of a stupid movie!

6. When we sob, we cry and gulp for air at the same time. We can sob quietly or loudly.

7. We think of weddings as joyous, happy occasions, but people often shed a few tears. Some of the wedding guests might silently shed a tear because they remember the bride and groom when they were children and it seems like such a short time ago. In the United States, the mother and father of the bride might quietly shed a tear or two because they don't know how they're going to pay for the wedding!

8. Marta was happy. She had just gotten a letter from her boyfriend. However, as soon as Marta finished reading the letter, she burst into tears. Her boyfriend wrote that he never wanted to see her again. She was heartbroken.

9. A three-year-old boy was playing outside with a friend. He started to howl. His mother could hear him even though she was in the house. She thought something really awful had happened to him, but he was howling only because his little friend had taken his favorite toy away from him.

The CRY Domain

Neutral

_____ cry _____

_____

_____

Silently

_____

Quietly

_____

Loudly

_____ wail _____

_____

Suddenly

_____

For a long time

_____

■ *Informal*

_____

Here is how the domain should look when you finish:

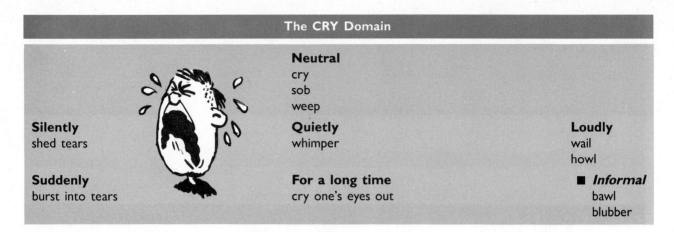

The CRY Domain

Neutral
cry
sob
weep

Silently
shed tears

Quietly
whimper

Loudly
wail
howl

Suddenly
burst into tears

For a long time
cry one's eyes out

■ *Informal*
bawl
blubber

VI. Exercises

The CRY Domain

Exercise 8: Sense or Nonsense?

Decide whether each sentence below makes sense or is nonsense. Circle the appropriate word. Remember, you may not agree with your classmates.

1. Some people in the United States sob at weddings.   SENSE   NONSENSE

2. Miriam lost one of her pencils. She cried her eyes out for several days.   SENSE   NONSENSE

3. A child is more likely to shed tears than an adult.   SENSE   NONSENSE

4. I might whimper if it was a bright sunny day and I got a good grade on my English test.   SENSE   NONSENSE

5. Children sometimes burst into tears when their parents tell them they can't have a new toy.   SENSE   NONSENSE

6. Some people wail when they are very distressed or unhappy.   SENSE   NONSENSE

7. If I won a million dollars in the lottery, I would start bawling.   SENSE   NONSENSE

Exercise 9: Matching

Part A

In the exercise that follows, a situation is described that might cause you to cry. Think about the situation, and then choose a verb from the list below to describe how you would react in that situation. Write it on the line.

shed tears   burst into tears   sob   wail   cry your eyes out

1. The main character in the movie you are watching is about to die.   1. _____

2. Your wallet is stolen while you are visiting New York City and now you have no more money.   2. _____

3. Your grandmother died yesterday. You loved her very much. You have been crying off and on ever since you heard the news.

3. _____

Part B

Individually or in a small group, create three more situations that might cause someone to cry. Be ready to read your description of each situation aloud. Your classmates will then choose a verb from the domain that fits the situation.

Exercise 10: Sentence Completion

Read each sentence below and decide how Sam or Susan reacted. Complete the sentences by writing the best word from the SMILE–LAUGH or the CRY domain on the line. Be prepared to explain your choice. Go back to pages 36 and 44 if you need to.

1. Sam really enjoys watching old silent movies. He __?__ with laughter during every one of Charlie Chaplin's films.

1. _____

2. Sam and Susan were at a party. When Susan finished telling a joke, Sam __?__ .

2. _____

3. One of Sam's friends died in the Vietnam War. When Sam saw a movie about this war, he was reminded of his friend and he __?__ .

3. _____

4. When Sam heard that Susan had been seriously injured in a car accident, Sam started to __?__ .

4. _____

5. Sam doesn't like his boss very much. One day, when Sam's boss made an embarrassing mistake in front of several employees, Sam __?__ .

5. _____

6. Susan quietly __?__ as she watched a heartbreaking TV show on homelessness.

6. _____

7. Sam and some of his friends were at a nightclub. They __?__ at the entertainer's jokes.

7. _____

8. Sam is very concerned about environmental issues. He was happy to read that an oil company had agreed to pay 50 million dollars to clean up an oil spill. He couldn't help __?__ as he read the article.

8. _____

9. Sam had some spinach quiche and then went to visit Susan. When he smiled at her, she started to __?__ because he had spinach between his teeth!

9. _____

VII. Expanding the Domain

> ### Figurative Meanings

Look at the following cartoon. Marvin, the baby in the cartoon, is crying because he spilled his milk. Therefore, to say that he is crying over spilled milk is a very literal use of this expression. This means he is crying because he really spilled his milk.

However, we usually use this expression figuratively. For example, if you get a bad grade on a test, you might feel bad. You might complain about it even

though it is too late to do anything. You are "crying over spilled milk." In fact, your friends might tell you to stop crying over spilled milk, and just study harder for the next test.

We could also call Marvin a crybaby, both literally and figuratively. He is a baby who is crying about his milk. He is also unhappy and complaining about something that has already happened.

Exercise 11: For Writing

Read the following dialogue with a partner. Then in a group or individually write your own short dialogue using don't cry over spilled milk and/or crybaby.

Kim and her older sister are talking. Kim is nine years old, and Iris is fifteen.

Kim: I wish I had studied more for my spelling test. I would have gotten a B if I had just studied last night.

Iris: Come off it. Don't cry over spilled milk. Just study harder for the next test.

Kim: But I know that the teacher thinks I'm stupid! She'll probably lower my grade. If I don't pass the fourth grade, Mom and Dad will be really angry!

Iris: Oh, stop it! You're being such a crybaby. Why don't you grow up?

Exercise 12: For Discussion

1. Tell a joke to your class or to a group of students in your class. Did they laugh? How did they laugh?

2. The title of this unit is "Laugh and the World Laughs With You, Cry and You Cry Alone." This is a well-known saying in English. In your own words, tell what you think it means. Is there a similar saying in your own language?

Do you know any other sayings in English or from your own culture about LAUGH or CRY?

Building
a New World

THE BUILD DOMAIN

I. Getting Ready

The world as we know it is constantly changing. Some of these changes are caused by nature. Others are the result of human effort. People establish new world organizations, build new kinds of houses, and create more fuel-efficient cars. Discuss the following questions with your whole class or in a small group.

1. Can you name some important world organizations that have been established in the 20th century?
2. How can someone build a more energy-efficient house?
3. What are the names of some companies that are making more fuel-efficient cars? How are cars made more fuel-efficient?

II. Introducing the Domain

The words establish, build, make, and create all refer to activities that result in something new. These and other words in this domain are given in the chart below. Look over the chart and mark the words that you don't know.

The BUILD Domain

Establish	Build		Make	Create
establish	build		make	create
found	construct		produce	invent
set up	erect		manufacture	think up
organize	put up		assemble	think of
			put together	come up with
			piece together	

III. Exploring the Domain

A. Verbs like establish, found, set up, and organize are used to describe the first step in starting a new company, an organization, or even a country.

The United States became an independent country in 1776. It was founded by people who didn't want America to be a British colony. It was set up on democratic principles. George Washington was one of the people who helped organize this new government. In fact, he served as the first U.S. President.

Do you know when your native country was established?

> establish
> found
> set up
> organize

B. Some words in this domain give the idea of people working on a building, a bridge, or some other physical structure. Some verbs like this are: build, construct, erect, and put up. We can say that the Berlin Wall was erected in 1961 to separate East and West Berlin. East German soldiers constructed the wall with barbed wire and bricks. Later, they put up huge walls of concrete. The Wall was torn down

> build
> construct
> erect
> put up

Constructing the Berlin Wall.

28 years after it was built. People in both East and West Germany wildly celebrated the end of "The Wall!"

Do you know why the Berlin Wall was erected?

C. The verbs make, produce, and manufacture are general words that describe the whole process of making a new thing. These are the words that you find printed on many man-made objects. For example, if you look on the bottom of a telephone you might find the words, "Manufactured in Singapore," or "Made in U.S.A." Look at the pen or pencil you are using today. Can you tell where it was produced? We use the verbs assemble, put together, and piece together to describe the action of making a new object out of separate parts or components. On a TV set, you might find the words "Assembled in U.S.A. with components from U.S.A. and other countries." This means that some of the parts were manufactured in other countries and shipped to the U.S.A. Then these parts were pieced together or put together. This process often takes place on an assembly line. Each person on the assembly line performs one step in the whole manufacturing process. These activities can be very boring and companies often use robots to do jobs that must be repeated many times.

What are some other advantages of using robots to manufacture products? What are some disadvantages?

| make |
| produce |
| manufacture |
| assemble |
| put together |
| piece together |

D. To <u>create</u> is to make something new that never existed before. <u>Scientists</u> and inventors do experiments and <u>create</u> new things. They <u>come up with</u> new solutions to old problems or they <u>think up</u> a completely new way of doing something.

People sometimes confuse <u>inventing</u> something new with discovering something. To discover something is to find out facts about the world and how it works. Thomas Edison didn't discover electricity, but he did <u>think of</u> new ways to use it. He <u>created</u> or <u>invented</u> many things that use electricity. One of his most famous <u>inventions</u> was the light bulb. Although Thomas Edison <u>invented</u> the light bulb, we can't say that he discovered it.

create
invent
think up
think of
come up with

IV. Exercises

Exercise 1: Beginning Practice

Cross out the underlined word in each sentence and write another word from the domain in its place. Pay attention to verb forms.

Example: The National Museum of African Art in Washington, D.C. was ~~built~~ _?_ in 1988.

Ex. _constructed_

1. The Great Pyramid in Egypt was <u>built</u> _?_ in 2590 B.C.

1. _____

2. Who <u>created</u> _?_ the light bulb?

2. _____

3. The U.S.A. was <u>established</u> _?_ as a country in 1776.

3. _____

4. When something is <u>made</u> _?_ in large quantities, its quality is sometimes reduced.

4. _____

5. Who <u>created</u> _?_ the cartoon character "Mickey Mouse?"

5. _____

6. When was the Eiffel Tower <u>built</u> _?_ ?

6. _____

7. How long does it take to <u>make</u> _?_ a car?

7. _____

8. Do you know when the first university in your country was <u>established</u> _?_ ?

8. _____

Exercise 2: Sentence Completion

Read the following sentences about various cultural and technological achievements. Choose the word that best completes each sentence and write it on the line.

1. The first wheel was _?_ in 3,500 B.C. (_founded, invented_)

1. _____

2. The Great Pyramid was _?_ at Giza in Egypt. (_erected, organized_)

2. _____

3. Paper was first ? in China. (*manufactured, constructed*)

3. _____

4. The first stone bridge was ? over the Tiber River in 142 B.C. (*produced, built, come up with*)

4. _____

5. The idea for the first watch was ? by someone in Nuremburg, Germany. (*established, set up, thought of*)

5. _____

6. The Red Cross was ? in 1864. (*pieced together, erected, organized*)

6. _____

7. The first photographic image was ? in 1822. (*established, assembled, produced*)

7. _____

8. Harvard, the oldest university in the U.S., was ? in 1636. (*founded, manufactured, thought up, produced*)

8. _____

9. Computers must be ? in clean, dust-free areas. (*founded, assembled, thought up, put up*)

9. _____

10. Henry Ford ? assembly lines to produce the Model T Ford. (*set up, manufactured, erected*)

10. _____

Exercise 3: For Discussion or Writing

Read the following paragraphs. Then, individually or in groups, answer each question.

A. Liberia is a West African country. It was set up as a colony for freed American slaves in 1822. It was organized by the American Colonization Society. In 1847, Joseph Jenkins Roberts, an American black man from Virginia, took over Liberia and established it as an independent country. He also served as its first president.

1. When was your native country established as an independent country?

2. Did a person or group of people found your country? Can you name them?

3. What city was set up as the first capital? Is it still the capital?

4. Has your country's system of government changed very much since it was first organized?

Liberia

B. One of the world's most famous structures is the Eiffel Tower. It was erected in 1889, exactly 100 years after the French Revolution. The man who designed it and built it was named Alexandre Eiffel. The tower he constructed has become the world-famous symbol of Paris and of France. While the workers were putting up the tower, Eiffel probably never imagined, even in his wildest dreams, that it would become so famous.

1. Can you think of another famous structure? To learn about it, talk to other students, or check in a dictionary or encyclopedia. When was it erected? Did it take a long time to build?

2. What kinds of buildings are being put up in your city now?

C. This is a recent headline from an American newspaper: "U.S. Workers Make Great Foreign Cars." In the 1980s, while car sales in the U.S. were generally decreasing, sales of Japanese cars in the U.S. were increasing. The fact is that more and more Japanese automakers are producing cars in the U.S. In fact, they manufacture more than a million cars every year. Even though these cars are assembled by American workers, the cars seem to be just as popular as those put together by Japanese workers in Japan.

1. What kinds of products are made in your country? Which ones are exported to other countries?

2. Companies are often looking for cheaper ways to manufacture their products. They may send the individual parts of a product to another country to be assembled. Why do you think this happens? What do you think of this business practice?

3. What do you know about assembly lines in your country? Is it more common for them to use people or robots to piece together products?

D. Coming up with new ideas and inventions requires imagination, curiosity, and good problem-solving skills. It isn't easy to create something that has never existed before. Inventing something often requires looking at ordinary objects in a different way. For example, one young inventor created a "jar of plenty." This is a simple, ordinary jar, but instead of having just one lid, it has two—one on each end. This makes it much easier to get to the food at the bottom of the jar!

1. What do you think is the most important invention of the 20th century? Why and when was it created?

2. In a group, try to come up with a new idea for how to use a simple, everyday object. For example, what are some new ways you could use a pencil? Or a paper clip?

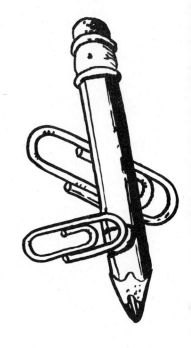

Exercise 4: Reading

Part A

Skim the following passage to find out more about Thomas Alva Edison, the man who invented the light bulb. As you read, underline the words from the domain.

Thomas Alva Edison: Inventor

Thomas Alva Edison, the American inventor, was born in 1847. Even as a child, he was always curious and always trying to invent new things. He was not a good student in school, but by the time he was a teenager, he had already had several jobs: store owner, telegraph operator, and inventor. He also had done lots of chemistry experiments on his own.   5

However, what Edison really wanted to do was research. He established his first laboratory in Menlo Park, New Jersey, and later he set up another one in West Orange, New Jersey. In these laboratories, he enjoyed trying to come up with solutions to problems that no one else had been able to solve.

One of his most exciting and difficult challenges was to create the electric light bulb. Today, it's very simple and easy to produce thousands of light bulbs a day. But Edison and his assistants had to work night and day to come up with just the right materials to make the first working light bulb. They tried over a thousand times to put together the right metals to create an electric bulb that would work for more than just a few seconds.

Once Edison had created this first working electric light, he came up with a way to produce light bulbs in quantity. His dream was to light up all of New York City. With this goal in mind, he constructed the world's first commercial electric power plant on Pearl Street in New York City.

As electric lighting became more and more popular, Edison had to find a way to measure the amount of electricity his customers were using. This is why he created the first electric meter. In 1878 he founded the Edison Electric Light Company. He also set up other companies that manufactured the bulbs and produced the motors that generated the electricity.

It wasn't long before several other businessmen set up their own electric companies to compete with Edison's companies. In fact, by 1890, six different electric companies had been established. One of the problems in having all these different companies was that they produced lights and equipment according to different standards.

This problem was solved in the 1880s when many of these companies joined together and organized a few large companies that mass-produced all electrical equipment according to the same standards. The outcome of all this was that Edison lost control of the companies he had originally set up. This didn't stop him, however. He continued inventing things. In fact, he went on to invent the phonograph (or record player) and he improved techniques used in the making of the first motion pictures.

When Edison died in 1931, he wasn't as rich as he could have been, but he was very famous. Many people were inspired by his story. He wasn't successful as a student in school, but that didn't stop him. He used his incredible intelligence and curiosity to create hundreds of inventions in his lifetime.

Thomas Alva Edison.

Part B

Go back and read the passage about Thomas Edison more carefully. Then answer these questions.

1. Why did it take Edison and his assistants such a long time to create the first working lightbulb?

2. Where was the first commercial electric power plant constructed?

3. What happened in 1878?

4. What happened twelve years later?

5. What was one of the problems with the first electric companies?

6. In your opinion, why wasn't Edison very rich when he died?

V. Expanding the Domain

Noun Forms

Most of the words in the BUILD domain have related noun forms. Let's look first at nouns that refer to the person who invents, makes, builds, etc. Notice that they all end in *-er* or *-or.*

Verb (the action)	Noun (the person who does it)
found	founder
organize	organizer
build	builder
construct	construction worker
make	maker
produce	producer
manufacture	manufacturer
assemble	assembler, assembly line worker
create	creator
invent	inventor

Exercise 5: Word Choice

Here is a list of characteristics that the people in the chart above might have. Individually or in a group choose two characteristics that a successful person in each category is most likely to have. Write these words on the lines. Your teacher may ask you to discuss your answers with the whole class.

imaginative	well-organized	rich	happy
curious	fearless	powerful	open-minded
intelligent	careful	energetic	creative
hardworking	physically strong	mentally strong	

1. A successful founder of a company is usually

   _____ and _____ .

2. A good assembly line worker should be _____

   and _____ .

3. A good inventor must be _____ and

   _____ .

4. A successful organizer is often _____ and

   _____ .

5. A construction worker should be _____ and

   _____ .

Construction workers rebuilding a pier.

English also has nouns that refer to the thing that is created, made, built, or established. Some of them are given below. Note that some of these words have the suffix *-ion*.

a building   an establishment   an invention   a product
a creation   a foundation   an organization

Exercise 6: Word Choice

Here is a list of well-known objects. Which of the nouns above would best characterize (describe) these objects? In some cases, more than one of the nouns may be correct.

Example: The United Nations _____ an organization _____

1. the Taj Mahal _____

2. a television set _____

3. a Mickey Mouse toy _____

4. the Red Cross _____

5. a painting by Picasso _____

6. a cotton t-shirt _____

7. the Kremlin _____

8. the Toyota Company _____

9. a Toyota _____

10. the electric motor _____

The United Nations.

Exercise 7: Sentence Completion

Choose the correct word to complete the sentence and write it on the line.

1. When was the United Nations __?__ (*established, establishment*)

2. What company is the best known __?__ of television sets? (*manufacture, manufacturer, manufacturing*)

3. A popular saying in English is, "Necessity is the mother of __?__ ." (*invention, inventor, invented*)

4. Good parents try to encourage their children to be __?__ . (*creation, creative, create*)

5. Ford is the __?__ of many different cars and trucks. (*product, producer, produce*)

6. Martin Luther King was one of the __?__ of nonviolent protests for civil rights in the U.S. (*organizers, organize, organizations*)

7. That department store sells many fine __?__ for the home. (*produce, production, products*)

1. _____

2. _____

3. _____

4. _____

5. _____

6. _____

7. _____

Exercise 8: For Discussion or Writing

Discuss and/or write your answers to one or more of these questions.

1. What are some dangers construction workers have to face?

2. Imagine you are going to give a prize to the founder of an important organization or university. Who would you give it to? Why?

3. Who was one of the most important inventors in human history?

The Big Picture About Size

THE BIG—LITTLE DOMAIN

I. Getting Ready

Living things come in all different sizes. Some are large, some are small, and some are in-between. We know from looking at prehistoric dinosaur bones that these animals were very large. On the other hand, there are millions of micro-organisms which are so small that we cannot see them without the help of a microscope.

Discuss the following questions with your whole class or in a small group.

1. Have you ever read a story or seen a movie about a person or animal who was very large? How big was this person or animal?

2. What are some very small living things that we can only see with the help of a microscope?

II. Introducing the Domain

There are many words in English that we use to talk about size. Some of these words are on the facing page. Look at the size of the words themselves. Which ones are the biggest? Which ones are the smallest?

Working by yourself or in a group, arrange these words according to their size. Put the words under the four headings below to create part of the BIG—LITTLE domain.

Very Big	Big	Little	Very Little

Here is how the BIG—LITTLE domain should look. In addition to the words you have just written, other, informal words have been added. Look over the chart of the domain and mark any words that you don't know.

The BIG—LITTLE Domain

Very Big	**Big**	**Little**	**Very Little**
very big	big	little	very little
huge	large	small	very small
gigantic		tiny	infinitesimal
giant		miniature	microscopic
enormous		petite	minute
immense			miniscule
monstrous			

■ *Informal* (Very Big)
humongous
giant-sized

■ *Informal* (Little)
pint-sized
itsy-bitsy
teeny

III. Exploring the Domain

Read the following passages and underline all the words that you can find from the domain.

A. How big is the biggest house you have ever seen? Some people like to have a really big house because they see it as a sign of their success.

   Let's look at Gino and Amelia's house. It's big! The living room is so enormous that you can play soccer on one side, basketball on the other, and still have room for an audience in the middle. Well, maybe this is an exaggeration, but it really is a huge house. The kitchen is so gigantic that six people can cook in it at the same time. The garage is so immense that you can put four cars in it. The front lawn is monstrous. It must take hours to mow it. Some people might say it's a waste of resources for four people to live in such a gigantic house.

B. How small is the smallest apartment you have ever seen? Let's look at Lan's apartment. She's petite and so is her apartment! It is called an efficiency apartment, which means that the living room, dining room, and bedroom are all in one small area. The kitchen is tiny. It has a small refrigerator and stove and a little table where she can eat her meals. She's thinking about buying a miniature dog for her little apartment.

C. Have you ever looked at something through a microscope? What did you see?

   Scientists use powerful microscopes to study viruses because these very tiny organisms are so miniscule. It is impossible to see them with our eyes. They are so infinitesimal that thousands of them would fit on the head of a pin. Although viruses are minute in size, they can be

very dangerous. They cause many illnesses from the common cold to some types of cancer. Who would think that these microscopic cells could cause so much trouble?

IV. Exercises

Exercise 1: Beginning Practice

Cross out the underlined words in each phrase below. Choose another word from the domain and rewrite the whole phrase on the line. Be careful with the articles *a* and *an*. Try to use as many different words as you can.

Example: a ~~very big~~ crowd

Ex. <u>an enormous crowd</u>

1. a <u>really big</u> house

1. _____

2. a <u>really small</u> bug

2. _____

3. a <u>very small</u> piece of dust

3. _____

4. the <u>little</u> hands of a newborn baby

4. _____

5. a <u>really big</u> whale

5. _____

6. a <u>very big</u> car

6. _____

7. a <u>very little</u> virus

7. _____

8. a <u>small</u> person

8. _____

9. a <u>very large</u> tree

9. _____

10. a <u>really large</u> theater

10. _____

Exercise 2: Sentence Completion

Complete the sentences with a word from the domain.

1. _____

1. In the 1950s, when gas was cheap, American cars were <u> ? </u> . They were so <u> ? </u> that six people could sit comfortably in them. But today most Americans buy <u> ? </u> cars that use less gas.

_____

_____

2. It is difficult to build a good telescope. Even <u> ? </u> imperfections in the lenses can cause problems.

2. _____

3. Eva is so <u> ? </u> that she has a hard time finding clothes that are small enough for her.

3. _____

4. Many children like to play with doll houses. A doll house is a <u> ? </u> version of a real house. The children enjoy putting <u> ? </u> plastic people and pieces of furniture in the house.

4. _____

_____

5. The first computers were ___?___ . Some of them filled a whole room. Today's computers are much smaller because of silicon chips. A silicon chip is very small and contains thousands of ___?___ electronic circuits.

5. _____

_____

Exercise 3: Making Comparisons

Part A

When you stand next to an elephant, you feel small. But, if you bend over and look at an ant, you feel big. Size is relative. Think about the size of the two animals below and fill in the blanks. Try to use as many different words as you can.

1. In comparison to a whale, a dog is ___?___ .

1. _____

2. In comparison to a dog, an ant is ___?___ .

2. _____

3. In comparison to an ant, an amoeba is ___?___ .

3. _____

4. In comparison to an amoeba, an elephant is ___?___ .

4. _____

5. In comparison to a bee, a rhinoceros is ___?___ .

5. _____

6. Compared to a hippopotamus, a cat is ___?___ .

6. _____

7. Compared to a gorilla, a squirrel is ___?___ .

7. _____

8. Compared to a fly, a giraffe is ___?___ .

8. _____

Part B

Look around your classroom. Write some sentences to compare some of the things you see.

Exercise 4: Looking at a Cartoon

Calvin and Hobbes

by Bill Watterson

Part A

Calvin and Hobbes is a popular American comic strip about a six-year-old boy who has many imaginary adventures. He often changes his size and shape. Answer the following questions about the cartoon.

1. How is Calvin doing his homework? Is he doing it speedily or leisurely?

2. Calvin has an excellent imagination. What is he imagining in this cartoon?

Part B

Describe the cartoon by completing the sentences with words from the domain.

Calvin is __(1)__ . Because he is so __(2)__ , it takes __(3)__ Calvin, the human insect, ten minutes to walk across each __(4)__ page! At the other end, he slowly lifts the __(5)__ sheet of paper! Then it's another trip back over the __(6)__ page as he turns it over!

1. _____   4. _____

2. _____   5. _____

3. _____   6. _____

Exercise 5: Reading

Part A

There are many stories about people who are much bigger or smaller than normal-sized people. For example, "Tom Thumb" is a well-known story about a little boy who was the size of a thumb. Another famous story, "Jack and the Beanstalk," is about a giant. Read and enjoy this familiar tale.

Jack and the Beanstalk

Once upon a time, there was a poor widow who lived in a tiny house with her only son, Jack. The winter had been so hard and cold that the poor woman decided to sell her cow to buy food for herself and Jack. She told Jack to take the cow to the market. On the way he met a farmer who had some beans. The farmer told Jack they were magic beans. Jack was a simple boy and it was 5 easy for the farmer to convince Jack to exchange the big, healthy cow for the tiny, little beans.

Jack ran home excitedly to show his mother the magic beans. She was very angry. "How could you do this? Now we have no cow—and no money to buy food!" She took the beans and threw them out the window. 10

The next morning, when Jack looked out the window, he was amazed to see an enormous beanstalk. It reached up into the clouds. Jack wasted no time. Without even telling his mother, he started climbing up the monumental beanstalk. When he reached the top, he found himself in front of an immense castle.

After the long climb, he was feeling hungry and tired. He went up to the 15 huge castle door and knocked. A kind woman answered the door and told him to come in. She told him to be very quiet because her husband, a giant, liked to eat children.

She hid Jack in a closet in the kitchen and told him to wait. Jack soon heard the heavy footsteps of the giant's enormous feet. "Fee, fi, fo, fum! I smell 20 the blood of an Englishman!" shouted the giant. The giant's wife told him that he had probably just smelled the delicious beef stew that she was making.

From inside the closet, Jack heard the giant sit down at his monstrous table and begin pounding his gigantic fists. "I'm hungry! Bring me my dinner!" he yelled to his wife. His wife quickly brought him some stew and the giant ate 25 and ate from his huge bowl and drank and drank from his giant-sized wine glass. Then he called to his wife, "Bring me my hen that lays the golden eggs!" His wife brought the hen and the giant watched as it laid dozens of big, beautiful golden eggs.

The giant had eaten and drunk so much that he started to feel very sleepy. 30 Before long, Jack could hear the giant snoring. The hen that laid golden eggs was still sitting on the table. She settled into her nest.

The giant's wife quietly opened the kitchen closet and let Jack out. She fed him some stew in a tiny bowl. The kind woman wanted to do something good for someone, so she told Jack to take the golden hen back to his mother. 35

As soon as Jack picked up the hen, it started to cry out. Jack hurried out the door with the hen under his arm and he started down the beanstalk. The noisy hen woke up the giant. "Fee, fi, fo, fum! I smell the blood of an Englishman!"

With huge strides, the giant ran out the door and saw tiny Jack hurrying 40 down the beanstalk. The giant started down after him. Jack hurried down as fast as he could. It was easy for him because he was so small. It was much harder for the immense giant.

When Jack got to the bottom of the beanstalk he quickly handed the golden hen to his surprised mother. He took a large ax and began to cut down the 45

---

gigantic beanstalk. The heavy giant quickly fell to his death.

Needless to say, Jack and his mother and the golden hen lived happily ever after!

Part B

Do *one* of the following writing assignments. Use as many of the words from the domain as possible in your writing.

1. Write a brief summary of "Jack and the Beanstalk."

2. In your native country is there a story in which the main character is not of normal size or changes size? Write a brief summary of the story.

V. Expanding the Domain

Prefixes Indicating Size

The prefixes in the box below are often used to indicate that something is large or small.

Large	Small
maxi-	mini-
macro-	micro-

Exercise 6: Sentence Completion

Choose the best word to complete the sentence and write it on the line.

microwave	mini-domain
microfilm	macrocosm
mini-van	microcosm
mini-skirt	

1. A very short skirt is called a __?__ .   1. _____

2. A small van is called a __?__ .   2. _____

3. A short electric wave that can be used to cook food is called a __?__ .   3. _____

4. A small group of related words could be called a __?__ .   4. _____

5. A special film that photographs pages and letters in a small size is called __?__ . 5. _____

6. The entire world can be called a __?__ .   6. _____

7. A small world that is similar to something larger is called a __?__ .   7. _____

Exercise 7: For Discussion

Prefixes indicating size are often found in other words, as well. In a group or with your whole class discuss what you think the following words mean.

macroeconomics   microsurgery
microbiology   maximum
minimize   minimum
maximize

Do you know any other words that have these prefixes?

VI. Creating Your Own Domain

This might be a good time for you to look at Unit 18. It describes a special project you can do with word domains. You have already seen several domains. You have learned how they are organized. In Unit 18, you can create your own domain.

Home is Where the Heart Is

THE DWELLING DOMAIN

I. Getting Ready

The DWELLING Domain

From the earliest times, humans have created homes for themselves. People have lived in caves, in trees, and even underground.

As the 21st century approaches, humans continue to live in a great variety of places, from incredibly large and luxurious houses to small and miserable shacks.

Think about your own city. What kinds of places do people live in? Take 10 or 15 minutes to write about all the different kinds of housing that you can find in your city. Try to write about everything from the biggest living spaces to the smallest ones. In addition, write about the kinds of people that inhabit these different kinds of houses. Your teacher may ask you to share your writing in a small group.

II. Introducing the Domain

In English, <u>dwelling</u> is a general word for a place to live. In this domain, you will learn about how Americans organize different words for dwellings. The words in this domain are presented below. Look over the chart and mark the words that you don't know.

Types of Housing

GENERAL

HOUSES

house
townhouse or rowhouse
duplex

home
dwelling
residence

APARTMENTS

apartment
efficiency or studio
condominium or condo

APARTMENT BUILDING

apartment building
high-rise

Most expensive
palace
castle
mansion
villa

Most expensive

luxury { apartment
condominium
condo

Least expensive
shack
shanty
hut
hovel

Least expensive
low-income public housing
housing project
tenement

homeless shelter

III. Exploring the Domain

A. Home Sweet Home

Home means many things to many people. It represents more than just the place where we have dinner or sleep. It is a place where we feel comfortable and satisfied and "at home." In fact, we use the word "homey" to describe a warm, comfortable environment.

Dwelling and residence are more formal words, which are used in official descriptions of the places people live. On official forms you might find the question, "Where is your permanent residence?" As you read the following paragraphs, think about which dwellings you might feel most "at home" in.

> home
> dwelling
> residence

B. A House Is Not a Home

A house is a separate building for one family or group of people. It often has a yard around it. A duplex is two houses that are attached to each other. A townhouse or rowhouse is one house in a row of attached houses.

> house   duplex
> townhouse   rowhouse

C. A Palace for a King or Queen

Many people dream of living in the biggest and most beautiful house they can imagine. They want to live in a palace that is good enough for a king or queen! Some people would be overjoyed to live in a palace like that of King Louis the XVI at Versailles or in Buckingham Palace, the home of the Queen of England. A palace is a living space for royalty.

In the past, royalty and other nobility also lived in castles. This kind of dwelling was usually located in a high, protected place. Today, some people live in castles that have been repaired and modernized.

A mansion is a large, expensive house, and so is a villa.

> palace
> castle
> mansion
> villa

D. Apartment Living

A popular kind of dwelling all over the world is an apartment. One of the reasons that apartment buildings are such a popular style of housing is that a lot of people can live on one piece of land. It's a very efficient use of space.

Some apartment buildings are very tall like skyscrapers. These buildings are called high-rises. If you take the elevator to the top floor of a high-rise you can usually get a superb view of the city.

There are also different kinds of apartments. An efficiency or studio is the smallest kind of apartment. It sometimes has a kitchen, a bathroom, and one room that serves both as a living room and a bedroom.

A condominium or condo is an apartment that you can buy. One reason they are popular in the city is that they are often cheaper to buy than houses.

People who have enough money to live "a life of luxury" also buy condos and rent apartments. We call these fancy, expensive dwellings luxury apartments or luxury condominiums.

> apartment
> efficiency
> studio
> condominium
> condo
>
> apartment building
> high-rise
>
> luxury apartment
> luxury condominium
> luxury condo

E. Down and Out: Housing for the Poor

The conditions in poor neighborhoods become worse as more and more people move from the countryside to already crowded urban areas. Sometimes, the people in these neighborhoods are unemployed or can find only low-paying jobs. Because they are poor, many of these people do not have adequate housing. They live in small, poor dwellings.

In some parts of the world, poor people live in neighborhoods that are crowded with small houses. A miserable living space like this can be called a shack, a shanty, or a hut. A really miserable small house can be called a hovel. People who don't have much money also live in apartment buildings. A tenement is an older kind of apartment building. It is generally a crowded building whose interior is dirty and poor. Some poor people might get help from the government to pay their rent. Two names for government-supported housing in the United States are low-income public housing and a housing project.

> shack
> shanty
> hut
> hovel
>
> low-income public
>   housing
> housing project
> tenement

F. The Homeless

Then, of course, there are people who don't have any kind of home at all. They don't have enough money to buy a house or pay rent on an apartment. Although they don't have a permanent residence, they do need some place to stay, so more and more cities are constructing homeless shelters that provide a temporary, overnight dwelling for homeless people.

> homeless shelter

IV. Exercises

Exercise 1: Beginning Practice

Look at the pictures and label them with the appropriate words from this domain.

condominium   shanty   duplex   townhouse   house

Exercise 2: Rhyming Words

Find a word from the domain chart on page 68 that rhymes with the underlined word.

Example: I will never <u>roam</u>
From my lovely ___?___ .

Ex. _____home_____

1. I know a rich man from <u>Dallas</u>
Who lives like a king in a ___?___ .

1. _____

2. Let's get a big <u>shovel</u>,
To clean out this ___?___ .

2. _____

3. Juan's very rich now,
He'll never go <u>back</u>
To that tiny, dirty, tarpaper ___?___ !

3. _____

4. If your house needs <u>expansion</u>
You should buy a big ___?___ .

4. _____

5. We need a cat
Because there's a <u>brown mouse</u>
Who eats all the cheese
In our large, new ___?___ .

5. _____

6. He has a lot of skill and <u>proficiency</u>
From living so long in a tiny ___?___ .

6. _____

7. I feel very little <u>sentiment</u>
For that crowded, noisy ___?___ .

7. _____

8. If you think that climbing's a <u>hassle</u>
Don't live on a hill in a fortified ___?___ .

8. _____

Exercise 3: Word Choice

Choose a word from the domain to tell where you think these people might live.

1. A homeless person might live in a _____ .

2. The King of Spain lives in a _____ .

3. A famous actress might live in a _____ on

the French Riviera.

4. Three recent college graduates might live together in an

_____ while they are looking for jobs.

5. A poor farmer who has just moved to the city with his family might

live in a _____ .

6. People who have low-paying jobs and can't afford to pay all of their

rent might live in a _____ .

Exercise 4: For Discussion or Writing

Work individually or in a small group to complete these sentences.

  1. A mansion and a villa are similar because. . .

  2. An apartment and a condominium are different because. . .

  3. The best place to build a high-rise is. . .

  4. I would never want to live in a homeless shelter because. . .

  5. If I lived in a castle, I would. . .

Exercise 5: For Discussion

Your teacher will give each student or each group of students one of the words from the DWELLING domain. Make a list of as many **advantages** and **dis-advantages** as you can think of for living in this kind of dwelling. Then share your answers with the class.

V. Expanding the Domain

More Types of Dwellings

Part A

There are some informal expressions for dwellings. One of them is <u>place</u>. This is a neutral word that you can use for any kind of house or apartment.

You could invite a friend over to your condo, for example, by asking, "Why don't you come over to my <u>place</u> before we go out to dinner?"

A more negative informal word for a dwelling is <u>dump</u>. A <u>dump</u> is a dirty, often small, place to live. Suppose you were looking for a new apartment. You went into one where there were cockroaches all over the kitchen floor and the paint was coming off the walls. You might say, "This place is a real <u>dump</u>! I could never live here!"

Exercise 6: For Discussion

If you can, ask a native speaker for other informal words for this domain. Make a list of these words.

Part B

The early Native Americans in the United States lived in a kind of tent called a <u>teepee</u>. Eskimos in Alaska live in <u>igloos</u>, houses made from blocks of ice. We use both of these words in English.

Exercise 7: For Discussion

1. Can you think of other words that we use in English to refer to dwellings from other cultures or countries?

2. There are probably special kinds of housing in your native country, too. What are they called? Can you describe them for your class?

Part C

What happens when you travel? Where do you stay? Everybody would like to find a comfortable "home away from home." In most cities, you can find <u>motels</u> and <u>hotels</u>. These are places with rooms for travelers. The word <u>motel</u> comes from "motor hotel." These are places for travelers that also have parking for their cars. A <u>hotel</u> is usually taller than a <u>motel</u> and may even be a high-rise.

We usually think of an <u>inn</u> as a motel in the countryside. In the United States, an increasingly popular type of hotel is a <u>bed and breakfast</u>. This is usually a private home where a home-cooked breakfast is served in the morning. It may be in the city or the country.

Some vacation homes are on wheels. Many people enjoy camping and they go on vacation in their <u>camper</u> or <u>van</u>. Some <u>campers</u> are even equipped with a kitchen and a bathroom.

Many people enjoy going to the beach or to the mountains. You can usually find a small house to rent for a week or more. This kind of small vacation house is called a <u>cabin</u> or a <u>cottage</u>.

| hotel |
| motel |

| inn |
| bed and breakfast |

| camper   van |

| cabin   cottage |

A hotel.

A camper.

Exercise 8: Sentence Completion

Complete the sentences with the best word from the domain by writing it on the line. You will need to use the plural form of some of these nouns.

motel	camper
hotel	van
bed and breakfast	cabin
inn	cottage

1. Yellowstone National Park is a wonderful place to camp, but it's getting really crowded. More and more people go there in their ___?___ . They eat and sleep in them and drive them all over the park.

2. There are some beautiful, old houses in northern California that are now being used as ___?___ . If you stay in one, the owners will probably serve you a wonderful home-cooked breakfast.

3. The coast of Florida is full of ___?___ and ___?___ . Sometimes you have to pay more than $100 a night for a small room with a double bed.

4. Government leaders like to stay in fancy ___?___ when they are traveling across the country. However, when they have some free time, their favorite places "to get away from it all" are sometimes little ___?___ near beautiful lakes or rivers.

5. It has a fold-down bed, a small kitchen sink and refrigerator, a fold-up breakfast table and a tiny shower and toilet. It's an amazing ___?___ ! It's really like a miniature house on wheels.

6. My neighbor dreams of having a little ___?___ in the woods one day where she can fish and watch the sunset. Everything would be peaceful and quiet.

1. _____

2. _____

3. _____

   _____

4. _____

   _____

5. _____

6. _____

Exercise 9: For Discussion or Writing

In which one of the places from the DWELLING domain would you like to live? Would you prefer a cabin or a palace, a little townhouse or an apartment, or something else altogether? Why? Work in groups to discuss what you would like your ideal dwelling to look like. Where would it be? Who would live there with you? Then, write a description of this place, and share it with your classmates.

Exercise 10: Explaining Popular Sayings

The title of this unit is "Home Is Where the Heart Is." This is a well-known saying in English. Another saying involving this domain is "A house is not a home." In your own words, tell what you think these sayings mean. Are there similar sayings in your native language?

THE FREQUENCY DOMAIN

I. Getting Ready

Take a few minutes to do an informal survey about the daily routine of your classmates. Ask five people the following questions. Record their answers on the chart given below by putting checks under their responses. Discuss your results with other members of the class.

1. How often do you eat breakfast?
2. How often do you miss a class or a day at work?
3. How often do you go to the movies?

	Never	Rarely	Sometimes	Always
1. Eat breakfast				
2. Miss class or work				
3. Go to the movies				

II. Introducing the Domain

In English there are many words that tell how often something is done. We call them "adverbs of frequency." Adverbs and other expressions of frequency are listed below.

Look over the words and phrases below and mark the ones that you don't know.

Frequency Expressions

0% ← —— LESS OFTEN —— MORE OFTEN —— → 100%

Never	Rarely	Sometimes	Often	Always
never	rarely	sometimes	often	always
not ever	seldom	occasionally	usually	invariably
at no time	infrequently	at times	frequently	constantly
	hardly ever			continually
not under any	scarcely ever	(every) now and	generally	consistently
condition		then	in general	
not under any		now and again	as a rule	all the time
circumstances		(every) once in a		at all times
on no occasion		while	commonly	without fail
		every so often	ordinarily	on every occasion
		from time to time	routinely	night and day
		on occasion	regularly	morning, noon,
				and night
	sporadically		repeatedly	
	irregularly		more often than not	
			■ *Informal*	
			a lot	

III. Exploring the Domain

A. People are different and that makes life interesting. Wouldn't it be dull if everyone did everything the same way? Here are descriptions of several different kinds of people. They are not descriptions of real people, though. They are stereotypes. No one is exactly like any of the descriptions, but there is a little of each of them in all of us.

B. Some people are methodical. They always have a strict routine and follow it all the time. For instance, they invariably get up at the same time each day and go to bed at the same time each night. They eat at the same time every day without fail and constantly worry if they are not on time. People like this follow the same pattern morning, noon, and night and get very upset if anything changes their routine.
   Methodical people are never flexible. They don't ever enjoy variation. They wouldn't under any circumstances stay in bed for an extra hour in the morning and at no time would they agree to eat dinner a little later than usual. People like this are slaves to their daily routine and can be difficult to get along with.
   Do you know anyone like this?

C. Fortunately, there are other types of people as well. Some are more flexible and sometimes change their daily routine. For instance, they sleep late every now and then, when they are feeling sick or very tired. Flexible people skip meals at times, because they are busy and don't have time to eat. Now and again they have a late dinner. People who are flexible occasionally take a day off work to help a friend. Every so often they go to a movie.
   Do you know anyone like this? Do flexible people make good friends?

D. Some people are even more flexible. They often change their daily routine, just for fun. They usually get up when they feel like it and are frequently late to work. Such people routinely take time off from their jobs and more often than not think friends are more important than work. As a rule, fun-loving people like this get bored easily. They repeatedly change jobs. These people are generally very easygoing. We call them "laid back."
   Do you know anyone like this? What do you think about people like this?

E. Some people are totally disorganized. They don't have any routine in their lives at all. They rarely plan ahead and are seldom prepared for work or school. People like this scarcely ever get their work done on time. Because they rarely meet deadlines, they are infrequently promoted.
   What do you think of people like this? Would you like to work with someone like this?

F. Regardless of what kind of person you are, there are some things that you should do regularly. For instance, doctors tell us to exercise regularly. But few of us do.

Both Maria and Bonita want to get in shape. During a two-week period they kept a record of each time they exercised. Look over the chart and then read the sentences below.

Maria exercises nearly every other day. She exercises <u>regularly</u>. Bonita has an unpredictable exercise pattern. She exercises <u>irregularly</u> or <u>sporadically</u>. She exercises a few days in a row and then <u>skips</u> a number of days. Is this a good way to get in shape? What would her doctor say?

	1	2	3	4	5	6	7	8	9	10	11	12	13	14
Maria		✔		✔		✔			✔		✔		✔	
Bonita	✔	✔							✔			✔		

IV. Exercises

Exercise 1: Beginning Practice

Cross out the word or phrase that doesn't belong.

1. invariably   at all times   sometimes

2. regularly   hardly ever   infrequently

3. now and then   at all times   from time to time

4. irregularly   usually   commonly

5. at times   now and again   from time to time   in general

Exercise 2: More Practice

Add a word or phrase that is similar in meaning.

1. not ever, never, not under any circumstances,   1. _____

2. repeatedly, routinely, generally,   2. _____

3. constantly, without fail, night and day,   3. _____

4. a lot, commonly, frequently,   4. _____

5. all the time, consistently, continually,   5. _____

Exercise 3: Comparing Frequencies

Read the pairs of sentences below. Decide on the frequency of each activity or event. Write *L* (*less often*) or *M* (*more often*).

Example: __L__ (a) Susan never eats breakfast.

__M__ (b) Sarah sometimes eats breakfast.

_____ 1. (a) Linda rarely goes to the doctor.

_____ (b) Keiko goes to the doctor all the time.

_____ 2. (a) Bill calls his mother every so often.

_____ (b) Rudolf doesn't ever call his mother.

_____ 3. (a) José does his homework sporadically.

_____ (b) Juan does his homework every day without fail.

_____ 4. (a) Theresa is late for work on occasion.

_____ (b) Jill is invariably late for work.

_____ 5. (a) Armando generally has a sandwich for lunch.

_____ (b) Misao infrequently has a sandwich for lunch.

_____ 6. (a) Peter ordinarily finishes his work before bedtime.

_____ (b) Leon consistently finishes his work before bedtime.

_____ 7. (a) Some children miss school often.

_____ (b) Some children miss school from time to time.

_____ 8. (a) Mother continually complains about her job.

_____ (b) My sister complains about her job at times.

_____ 9. (a) Mrs. Chang routinely cleans her house in the spring.

_____ (b) I don't clean my house under any circumstances.

_____ 10. (a) After the accident, the police officer repeatedly asked the driver why he left his car in the middle of the road.

_____ (b) At no time after the accident did the police officer ask the driver why he left his car in the middle of the road.

Exercise 4: Comparing Frequencies

Part A

Can you compare three frequency expressions? Put *1* (the least frequent), *2* (the next most frequent), and *3* (the most frequent of all).

Example: rarely __1__ always __3__ occasionally __2__

1. hardly ever ___ on no occasion ___ usually ___

2. as a rule ___ invariably ___ at no time ___

3. now and again ___ without fail ___ scarcely ever ___

4. rarely ___ not ever ___ every so often ___

5. in general ___ infrequently ___ consistently ___

Part B: A Special Challenge

Now compare these expressions, using numbers 1–4. Try to do this without consulting the chart on page 76, then check your own answers.

1. seldom ___ invariably ___ at times ___ never ___

2. irregularly ___ repeatedly ___ on no occasion ___

   at all times ___

3. on occasion ___ night and day ___ seldom ___ not ever ___

Exercise 5: For Discussion

Part A

In a small group discuss which word or expression listed below is the most appropriate one for each situation. There may be more than one correct choice, so be prepared to discuss your answers.

> on no occasion   in general
> scarcely ever   at all times
> now and again

1. A soldier wears a uniform.   1. _____

2. It rains in the desert.   2. _____

3. Dogs growl at strangers.   3. _____

4. The sun rises in the west.   4. _____

5. When riding in a car you should wear your seatbelt.   5. _____

6. An airplane makes an emergency landing.   6. _____

7. Good students do their homework.   7. _____

8. A thief is caught and sent to jail.   8. _____

Part B

If you change the sentences above in some way, you might want to change the frequency expression, too. For example, if sentence 7 had the adjective <u>poor</u> instead of <u>good</u>, would you choose a different frequency expression? With your class or in a small group, change some of the sentences above. Then decide what frequency expression would be most appropriate.

Exercise 6: Word Choice

Decide how often *you* do these activities. Complete the sentences with the most appropriate expression from the FREQUENCY domain. Be honest!

You will have to add an auxiliary verb if the expression begins with the word <u>not</u>.

Example: I __?__ skip school __?__ . (*not under any circumstances, occasionally, always*)   **Ex.** <u>do not . . . under any circumstances</u>

1. I eat pizza __?__ . (*rarely, sometimes, a lot, all the time*)   1. _____

2. I __?__ smoke cigarettes. (*never, infrequently, often, continually*)   2. _____

3. I __?__ get good grades in school. (*not ever, ordinarily, consistently*)   3. _____

4. I watch TV __?__ . (*every now and then, a lot, night and day*)   4. _____

5. I __?__ go to concerts. (*hardly ever, occasionally, frequently*)   5. _____

6. I exercise or work out __?__ . (*not under any circumstances, sporadically, regularly*)   6. _____

7. __?__ I go to bed before midnight. (*Once in a while, In general, Invariably*)   7. _____

8. I drive above the speed limit __?__ . (*not under any condition, on occasion, more often than not*)   8. _____

9. I __?__ pay my bills on time. (*not ever, occasionally, routinely*)   9. _____

10. When I make a mistake, I admit it __?__ . (*not under any condition, on occasion, without fail*)   10. _____

Exercise 7: Sense or Nonsense?

Decide whether each of the sentences below makes sense or is nonsense to you. Then circle your choice.

1. It always snows at the North Pole.	SENSE	NONSENSE
2. Most volcanoes erupt infrequently.	SENSE	NONSENSE
3. Every now and then giraffes have long necks.	SENSE	NONSENSE
4. Hollywood movie stars hardly ever get divorced.	SENSE	NONSENSE
5. Some students attend class without fail.	SENSE	NONSENSE
6. The mail carrier delivers the mail once in a while.	SENSE	NONSENSE
7. As a rule the British have tea in the afternoon.	SENSE	NONSENSE
8. Americans stop at every red light without fail.	SENSE	NONSENSE
9. If you study sporadically, you'll be an excellent student.	SENSE	NONSENSE
10. You shouldn't eat meat and potatoes under any circumstances.	SENSE	NONSENSE
11. In general, if you heat a metal, it expands.	SENSE	NONSENSE
12. It is not healthy to watch TV morning, noon, and night.	SENSE	NONSENSE

Exercise 8: Reading

Part A

Read the following story as quickly as you can. Underline any words you find from the FREQUENCY domain. Then go back and read it again more carefully.

Miss Marbles

Miss Marbles is a sweet, old woman who lives at the edge of a village in England. She is always interested in everything around her. She frequently takes long walks through the village to check up on everything. She invariably notices things like a new flower bed or a newspaper left outside. She talks regularly to her neighbors and as a rule knows everything that is going on in the village.   5

But every now and then Miss Marbles gets upset about something and is not her usual, observant self. Last Friday was one of those times. She had lost her pocketbook and didn't know what to do. It was time for her weekly shopping and all her money was in her purse.

She hurried to the village square and didn't even notice the stranger following   10
her on the road. In the square she went from store to store, asking everyone about her pocketbook. The stranger was invariably a few steps behind her. Three or four times he actually followed her into the store and tried repeatedly to get her attention. On every occasion, she was busy asking about her pocketbook and didn't see him.   15

At noon Miss Marbles turned toward home. No one had seen her pocketbook. She was very depressed. "This hasn't ever happened to me before," she thought. "I so rarely lose anything. And I'm usually so careful with my purse."

As she trudged up the path to her house, the stranger was waiting for her. "Excuse me, ma'm," he mumbled. "Are you Miss Marbles?" 20

When she nodded "yes," he held something out to her and continued. "I believe this is your purse. I found it on the road and have been trying to return it to you all day."

Part B

Complete the sentences using the expressions from the FREQUENCY domain.

1. Miss Marbles is _____ observant.

2. _____ she gets preoccupied.

3. The man in the story _____ tried to get her attention.

Part C: For Discussion

1. How does Miss Marbles usually spend her time? What kinds of things does she do regularly? What kind of a person is she?

2. Do you know someone like Miss Marbles? Do you like this kind of person? Why or why not?

V. Expanding the Domain

Saying "No"

If someone asks you to go to a horror movie such as *Frankenstein* you could simply say "no" if you didn't want to go. But if you really detest horror movies, you might say <u>never</u>. <u>Never</u> is a stronger way of saying "no." Below are some informal expressions which are also strong ways to say "no" or "never." They are used only in casual, conversational English. We use expressions like these with close friends or family members.

not in a million years	no way, José
not on your life	when hell freezes over
no way	

The dialogue below shows how one of these informal expressions is used. The speakers are brothers, Tom, age 16 and Jerry, age 22.

Tom: Hey, Jerry, I just got my driver's license. Can I borrow your car for a week?

Jerry: Not in a million years. I'd never give my car to an inexperienced driver like you.

Exercise 9: Sentence Completion

With a partner read the following dialogues. Complete the sentences with one of the informal words or expressions for <u>never</u>.

Dialogue A

Jerry: I'm real busy today, Tom. Would you mow the lawn for me?

Tom: _____ . Not after you were so mean to me.

Dialogue B

Tom: Can I go to the movies with you and your girlfriend?

Jerry: _____ . We want to be alone!

Dialogue C

Tom: Can I use your VCR while you're at the movies tonight?

Jerry: _____ . You're so clumsy you'd probably break it.

Remember to be very careful using these expressions. You will sound rude or impolite if you use them inappropriately.

Exercise 10: For Discussion

Some informal English expressions for <u>never</u> refer to an extremely long time (<u>not in a million years</u>) and others refer to something that we suppose will never happen (<u>when hell freezes over</u>). What are some special expressions in your native language for saying "no" or "never"?

Exercise 11: Explaining Popular Sayings

The title of this unit is "Never say Never." This is a well-known saying in English. In your own words, tell what you think it means. Is there a similar saying in your native language? Do you know other sayings in English or your native language which use other expressions from the FREQUENCY domain?

Exercise 12: For Discussion or Writing

Look back at the descriptions of different people in "Exploring the Domain" (page 77). Then discuss one or more of these questions in a small group and/or write a short answer to share with the class.

1. Describe your daily routine.

2. What are some activities you do regularly? What are some things you like to do sporadically?

3. What kind of a person are you—methodical, easygoing, or totally disorganized? Which of the descriptions is most like you?

4. Most people have some characteristics of each of the people described in "Exploring the Domain." They are, for example, methodical about some things and very easygoing about others. Describe a person you know and the ways in which that person is like the people described in this section.

UNIT 10

It's Nature's Law TO CHANGE

THE CHANGE DOMAINS

In this unit you are going to learn verbs for change. Because there are so many verbs of change, they have been divided into three groups: change in physical size, change in quantity, and change in strength or speed.

I. Getting Ready

'Tis Nature's law to change,
Constancy alone is strange.

This saying means that things are continually changing. Change is inevitable. We can't stop it. Prices go up and down, planes travel faster and farther, the seasons change, and people grow older. Change is part of our lives.

Discuss the following questions with your whole class or in a small group.

1. What happens to a balloon when you blow air into it?
2. What happens to the number of fish in a lake that is becoming more and more polluted?
3. What do you do if you want to pass a car on the highway?

The questions above are about different kinds of change: change in physical size, quantity and speed. Can you think of another example of each kind of change?

II. Introducing the Domain

CHANGE in Physical Size

The verbs in the first domain indicate a change in physical size. They tell us that an object has gotten bigger or smaller. Look over the verbs below and mark the ones that you don't know.

CHANGE in Physical Size

Become Bigger	Become Smaller
get bigger	get smaller
grow	
enlarge	reduce
	shrink
expand	contract
	constrict
inflate	deflate
blow up	
widen	narrow
broaden	
heighten	
deepen	
lengthen	shorten

III. Exploring the Domain

The words in this domain are used by people in many different professions, from doctors to fashion designers. Doctors know that tension and stress can cause blood vessels to constrict, which can bring on a headache. They might prescribe a drug to expand the vessels.

A physics instructor teaches his students that heat causes some materials to expand and cold causes them to contract. If the instructor wants to fit a lot of information about expansion and contraction on one piece of paper, he or she might use a photocopy machine to reduce the page he is copying.

Photographers also reduce things. A large picture can be reduced to fit in someone's wallet. Photographers often enlarge photos to make small details easy to see.

Meteorologists, scientists who study weather, often send enormous weather balloons into the sky to learn about conditions high above the earth. They inflate or blow up these balloons to make them rise. When the balloons lose air or deflate, they fall back to the earth.

As more and more people use cars to commute to work, engineers broaden or widen roads. The people who live next to the new roads get angry when the engineers narrow their yards in order to widen the roads. Engineers also might have to deepen a harbor or heighten a bridge so that immense, ocean-going ships can enter the harbor.

Fashion designers often use the words lengthen and shorten, especially when it comes to skirts! One year they lengthen skirts so that they reach women's ankles, and the next year they shorten them into mini-skirts that don't even reach the knees. They also like to have fun with men's ties, widening them one year and narrowing them the next.

As we said at the beginning of this unit, change is a normal part of life. We can't stop it. It seems to be inevitable!

get bigger	get smaller
grow	
enlarge	reduce
	shrink
expand	contract
	constrict
inflate	deflate
blow up	
widen	narrow
broaden	
heighten	
deepen	
lengthen	shorten

IV. Exercises

Exercise 1: Beginning Practice

Study the words in this domain for a few minutes. Then, without looking at the chart, try to put each word from the list below into the correct column. When you have completed the exercise, look back at the chart on page 86 to see how well you did.

deflate	blow up	enlarge
shrink	broaden	reduce
inflate	shorten	expand
narrow	lengthen	widen
constrict	contract	deepen
grow	heighten	

CHANGE in Physical Size

Become Bigger	Become Smaller
_____	_____
_____	_____
_____	_____
_____	_____
_____	_____
_____	_____
_____	_____
_____	_____
_____	_____

Exercise 2: Word Choice

Choose the best word to complete the sentence and write it on the line.

1. If I wash a cotton T-shirt in hot water, it will __?__ . (*expand, shrink, get bigger*)

2. The windows in my house are too small. I want to __?__ them. (*shorten, enlarge, constrict*)

3. When I take a deep breath, I bring air into my lungs and they __?__ . (*expand, deflate, narrow*)

4. I can use a photocopy machine to __?__ a picture. (*reduce, deepen, heighten*)

5. When the muscles in my legs __?__ , my legs move. (*inflate, deflate, contract*)

6. Some balloons are difficult to blow up. You have to blow very hard to __?__ them. (*heighten, constrict, inflate*)

1. _____

2. _____

3. _____

4. _____

5. _____

6. _____

7. I am building a new desk for myself, but I think it is going to be too narrow. I'll __?__ it by adding another board. (*shorten, widen, shrink*)

7. _____

8. If you __?__ a hose, water can't flow through it. (*constrict, deflate, lengthen*)

8. _____

V. Introducing the Domain

Now let's look at verbs that express a change in quantity. These verbs tell us that the number or amount of something is becoming more or less. For instance, temperatures usually <u>rise</u> during the day and <u>fall</u> or <u>decrease</u> at night.

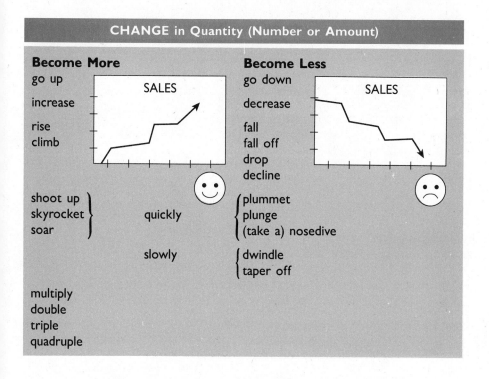

CHANGE in Quantity (Number or Amount)

Become More
go up
increase
rise
climb

shoot up ⎫
skyrocket ⎬ quickly
soar ⎭

slowly

multiply
double
triple
quadruple

Become Less
go down
decrease
fall
fall off
drop
decline

⎧ plummet
⎨ plunge
⎩ (take a) nosedive

⎧ dwindle
⎨ taper off

VI. Exploring the Domain

Part A

If you read an article in a newspaper or magazine, you will probably find many of these verbs of change. Read the article below. As you read, underline eight different verbs from the domain.

Health Care Costs in the U.S. Are Soaring

Since 1965, the amount of money spent on medical care in the U.S. has sky-rocketed. In some states the cost of buying health insurance for a family of four quadrupled from 1980 to 1990. If costs continue to shoot up, many Americans will not be able to afford good medical care. In the U.S., employers usually pay for medical insurance for their employees. But employers are afraid 5 that if the cost of this insurance continues to climb, they will not be able to pay for it without increasing the prices of their products. They hope that the big increases in the cost of medical care will taper off or dwindle in the near future.

What is happening to health care costs in your country?

Part B

The following article could be found in the business section of a newspaper or magazine. Read the article and underline seven verbs from the domain.

Economic Problems Multiply

Many economists feel the economy is in trouble. They are predicting that a recession (a period of slow economic activity) is on the way. Retail sales have declined because people are buying fewer new cars, clothes, and appliances. The number of new houses sold has plummeted to record lows. Because sales are decreasing, unemployment has begun to rise. All of this bad news has caused 5 the value of many stocks to take a nosedive and several companies are close to declaring bankruptcy. If exports are increased, will the economy improve? Or is a recession inevitable? Only time will tell.

What is happening to the economy in your country?

VII. Exercises

CHANGE in Quantity

Exercise 3: Beginning Practice

Study the words in this domain for a few minutes. Then, without looking at the chart, try to put each word from the list below into the correct column. When you have completed the exercise, look back at the chart to see how well you did.

climb	taper off
plunge	rise
increase	triple
dwindle	soar
plummet	go up
double	decrease
multiply	decline
fall off	shoot up
skyrocket	quadruple
drop	take a nosedive

CHANGE in Quantity (Number or Amount)	
Become More	**Become Less**
_____	_____
_____	_____
_____	_____
_____	_____
_____	_____
_____	_____
_____	_____
_____	_____
_____	_____
_____	_____
_____	_____
_____	_____
_____	_____
_____	_____

Exercise 4: Word Choice

Complete the sentences below with the most appropriate word from the CHANGE in Quantity domain. Be careful with verb forms.

1. Since 1980 the cost of living in my country has

   _____ .

2. Since 1900 the population of the earth has

   _____ .

3. In 1950 Jonas Salk discovered a vaccine for polio. Since then the

number of cases of polio has _____ .

4. Since 1980 the number of people who use computers in their jobs has

_____ .

5. Since 1970 the size of the average family in western countries has

_____ .

6. During the Great Depression, the number of unemployed workers

_____ .

7. In the 20th century, the number of independent nations has

_____ .

8. Recently, the number of people who worry about another world war

has _____ .

Exercise 5: Reading a Bar Graph

Use the information in the bar graph below to write four sentences about the population of the world. Use a different word from the CHANGE in Quantity domain in each sentence.

Example: The population of the world has <u>climbed</u> steadily since 1650.

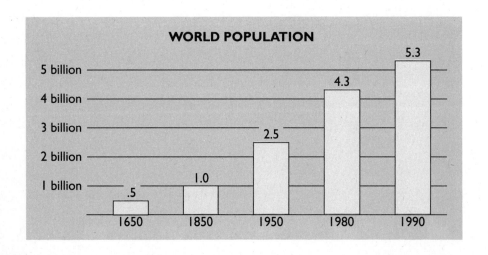

VIII. Introducing the Domain

CHANGES in Strength or Speed

This domain contains two groups of verbs. The verbs in the first group indicate a CHANGE in strength and those in the second group indicate a CHANGE in speed. Look at the chart below and mark the words that you don't know.

CHANGE in Strength

Make Stronger
strengthen
fortify
reinforce

Make Weaker
weaken
dilute
water down
undermine

CHANGE in Speed

Go Faster
accelerate
speed up

Go Slower
decelerate
slow down

IX. Exploring the Domain

CHANGES in Strength or Speed

Here are some examples of how these words are used.

Part A: Strength

1. You can strengthen your muscles by exercising regularly.
2. After the earthquake, many people had to reinforce the walls of their houses.
3. In the United States, most milk is fortified with vitamins A and D.
4. The chemist diluted or watered down the mixture by adding water to it.
5. The president of the company undermined the authority of his vice president by yelling at him in front of the workers.

Part B: Speed

6. When you step on the gas pedal, a car <u>accelerates</u>. When you step on the brake, the car <u>decelerates</u>.
7. We need to <u>speed up</u> the distribution of food to the hungry children of Africa.
8. Many people want to <u>slow down</u> the growth in the world's population.

X. Exercises

> **CHANGE in Strength or Speed**

Exercise 6: Beginning Practice

Cross out the word that doesn't belong.

1. fortify   dilute   reinforce

2. accelerate   slow down   decelerate

3. water down   dilute   strengthen

4. speed up   slow down   accelerate

5. undermine   strengthen   reinforce

Exercise 7: Word Choice

Choose the word that best completes the sentence and write it on the line.

1. This coffee is too strong for me. I'm going to __?__ it with some water. (*accelerate, fortify, dilute*)

   1. _____

2. In order to make the skyscraper even taller, the engineers decided to __?__ the walls. (*slow up, reinforce, undermine*)

   2. _____

3. Before airplanes can land they have to __?__ to a safe speed. (*speed up, decelerate, water down*)

   3. _____

4. Stress can cause the aging process to __?__ . (*accelerate, weaken, fortify*)

   4. _____

5. Hospital patients often have to stay in bed for many days. This __?__ their muscles. (*strengthens, reinforces, weakens*)

   5. _____

XI. Exercises

The exercises that follow will give you practice with all the verbs of change that you have learned in this unit: change in physical size, change in quantity, and change in strength or speed.

Exercise 8: Sentence Completion

Decide which kind of change is being described: change in size, quantity, speed
or strength. Then complete the sentences with a word from the correct domain.

1. When we breathe in, our lungs __?__ and when we breathe out,
   they __?__ .

1. _____

   _____

2. When a bicycle is going uphill it __?__ . When it is going downhill
   it __?__ .

2. _____

   _____

3. Doctors know that the number of children who get colds __?__ when
   they return to school in the fall.

3. _____

4. If pregnant women stopped smoking and drinking alcohol, the infant
   mortality rate would __?__ .

4. _____

5. In Washington, D.C., temperatures can __?__ to 100°F in August
   and __?__ to 10°F in February.

5. _____

   _____

6. A chemical reaction __?__ when the chemicals are heated and slows
   down when they are cooled.

6. _____

7. Heat causes metal to __?__ and cold causes it to __?__ .

7. _____

   _____

Exercise 9: Word Choice

Some people are never satisfied. They always want things to be bigger or smaller or to go faster or slower. Give advice to the complainers in these sentences. Tell them how to solve their problems.

Example: Carol thinks her vegetable garden is too small. She should ? it.

Ex. _____enlarge_____

1. Emilio thinks his family room is too narrow. He should ? it.

1. _____

2. Susan took a beautiful picture of her mother, but she thinks it's too small to hang on the wall. She should ? the picture.

2. _____

3. Lili thinks her son is driving too fast. She should tell him to ? .

3. _____

4. Claude's tea is too strong. He should ? it.

4. _____

5. Tony wants to impress the girls, but he thinks his muscles are too weak. He should ? them.

5. _____

6. Christina wants to wear her new skirt to the party, but she thinks it's too long. She should ? it.

6. _____

7. Azadeh wants to be able to dive into her swimming pool, but the pool is too shallow. She should ? it.

7. _____

8. Sarah is ashamed of her nose. She thinks it's too big. She could have surgery to ? the size of her nose.

8. _____

Exercise 10: Writing Sentences

Write a sentence that answers each question below.

1. Mr. and Mrs. Edwards have a four-year-old daughter. Yesterday Mrs. Edwards gave birth to twins. What happened to the number of children in their family?

2. If I work out with weights every day, what will happen?

3. The amount of money that people are giving to charities is dwindling. Is this good or bad? Why?

4. If 500 new houses are built, but only 450 families want to buy a new house, what will happen to the price of the houses?

5. If 500 new houses are built, but 600 families want to buy a new house, what will happen to the price of the houses?

6. If a male rabbit and a female rabbit are put in the same cage, what will happen to the number of rabbits?

Exercise 11: Charts and Graphs

In a newspaper or magazine, find a chart or a graph similar to the one in Exercise 5. Write four sentences that describe the changes indicated by your chart or graph. Use as many words from the domains as possible in your sentences.

Exercise 12: For Discussion

Because the world is constantly changing, the words from the three CHANGE domains appear often in newspapers and magazines. Bring in headlines from a newspaper or magazine that contain words from the CHANGE domains. Share them with the class.

XII. Expanding the Domain

Abstract Meanings

The words in the CHANGE domains don't always refer to changes in concrete, physical objects, such as a room that is enlarged or a chemical mixture that is diluted. Sometimes these words are used to talk about changes in things that are abstract, as in the sentence below.

Bad health habits like smoking and not exercising can <u>shorten</u> your life.

A life is not a concrete, physical object that we can touch. But we often talk about <u>shortening</u> a life in the same way that we talk about <u>shortening</u> a skirt.

Exercise 13: Concrete or Abstract?

Decide whether the underlined word is being used to describe a change in a concrete object or in an abstract one. Write *C* if the thing that is changing is *concrete* and *A* if it is *abstract*.

Example: ___A___ Julio took a class in inter-cultural communication. It <u>heightened</u> his awareness of other cultures.

_____ 1. Harry has a few simple problems. But he thinks that his problems are really serious. He <u>blows</u> them <u>up</u> all out of proportion.

_____ **2.** Mary's eyes <u>widened</u> in surprise as she listened to Peter's astonishing story.

_____ **3.** After graduation from college, Marshall wanted to <u>broaden</u> his horizons, so he joined the Air Force.

_____ **4.** My history teacher said my paper contained too many different ideas. She told me to <u>narrow</u> the focus of the paper by writing about only one main <u>idea</u>.

_____ **5.** Psychologists say that it is better to <u>reinforce</u> good behavior in children with rewards than to punish <u>bad behavior</u>.

_____ **6.** Wisconsin Avenue will soon be <u>widened</u> to three lanes.

_____ **7.** He thinks he's really smart. I'd like to see someone <u>deflate</u> his ego.

_____ **8.** Doctors can sometimes <u>shrink</u> tumors without surgery.

Some Like It Hot

THE HOT—COLD DOMAIN

I. Getting Ready

Temperature is important in our lives. In the United States, for example, people like their pizzas hot and their sodas very cold. They want their houses to be warm in winter and cool in summer.

Discuss the following questions with your whole class or in a small group.

1. Do people in your country like their drinks to be really cold? Do they like their food to be hot or only warm?
2. Have you ever been in a hot, stuffy classroom, listening to a teacher talk? Was it hard to concentrate on what the teacher was saying? Did you feel sleepy?
3. Have you ever been so cold that your fingers or your lips turned blue? Do you like being outside when it is really cold?

II. Creating the Domain

In this unit we are going to look at adjectives that describe temperature. Instead of giving you the domain, we're going to ask you to create it. Read the paragraphs on page 101. The underlined words and expressions all belong in the HOT–COLD domain. Using the information in the paragraphs, put the underlined words and expressions in one of the four columns below.

The HOT–COLD Domain			
Hot	**Warm**	**Cool**	**Cold**
_____	_____	_____	_____
_____	_____	_____	_____
_____	_____	_____	_____
_____			_____
_____			_____
_____			_____
_____			_____
_____			_____
_____			_____
_____			

A. You can find every possible kind of weather on our planet Earth. If you like hot temperatures, why not visit Phoenix, Arizona in the United States? The temperatures there are scorching during the day, sometimes getting as high as 120°F (49°C). This is certainly a fiery climate. During the summer the sidewalks in Phoenix are sizzling and some people say that you could fry an egg on them! But it is not always blistering there. At night, after the sun goes down, the temperature drops and it becomes quite cool. In fact, after the very hot temperatures of the day, evenings feel quite chilly.

The climate of Phoenix is hot, but it is also dry. If you prefer a climate that is hot and humid (with more moisture in the air), why not visit the Amazon jungle in South America? The weather there is steamy. Temperatures can reach 100°F (38°C) and humidity levels are very high.

If you prefer a warm, mild climate, the state of Hawaii might be the place for you. Because of the trade winds, the climate of Hawaii is mild all year. The temperature there is between 70°F (21°C) and 80°F (27°C) most of the year.

B. For those who like very cold, frigid weather, there's always Alaska. Freezing temperatures are common there for many months of the year. In Barrow, a city on the northern coast of Alaska, the average high temperature never gets above the freezing point (32°F, 0°C) for eight months of the year. The frosty air of Alaska makes some people feel energetic. They enjoy the wintry weather and don't seem to understand why other people find the glacial temperatures difficult to live with.

Some people find it boring to live in Hawaii or Arizona, where the weather is warm all year. They want to live in a place that has four seasons, four different kinds of weather. They like the icy days of winter, the mild days of spring, the scorching days of summer and the chilly days of fall. How about you?

C. A few words for hot are used mainly about liquids. Scalding means very hot and tepid means warm. For example, when coffee is very hot, we say it is scalding and when water is warm, we say it is tepid.

Another word used mostly about liquids is lukewarm. Bath water that is not hot and not cold is lukewarm.

The expression piping hot is also used for liquids or foods and means very hot. We might eat a piping hot stew or like to drink our coffee piping hot. Two other expressions which mean very hot use colors. When we say that something is red-hot or white-hot, we're saying that it is very hot.

D. In an informal conversation, an American might say stone cold or numb with cold to indicate that something or someone is very cold. We also say blue with cold, probably because our fingers or lips turn blue when they are very cold.

If you listen to an American TV show or movie, you might hear the expressions hot as hell or hotter than hell. These are slang expressions that mean very hot. But use them carefully. They are considered impolite by some people.

III. The HOT–COLD Domain

Now compare your lists with the chart of the HOT–COLD domain given below. This chart includes even more information about these words and should help you understand them better.

The HOT–COLD Domain

Hotter Than Hot	Hot	Warm	Cool	Cold	Colder Than Cold
scorching	hot	warm	cool	cold	freezing
blistering		◊ lukewarm	chilly		icy
sizzling		◊ tepid			glacial
steamy					wintry
red-hot					frosty
white-hot					frigid
piping hot					
fiery					■ *Informal*
					stone cold
◊ scalding					blue with cold
					numb with cold
■ *Informal*					
hot as hell*					
hotter than hell*					

*These words are slang; use them carefully.
◊ These words are used with liquids.

IV. Exercises

Exercise 1: Beginning Practice

Part A

Working with a partner, choose an adjective from the domain to describe each of these objects.

1. an ice cube

2. a burning log (piece of wood)

3. a 60°F (15°C) day

4. a 95°F (35°C) classroom

5. the Sahara desert

6. water that is 105°F (40°C)

7. an iron that is turned to "high"

8. hands that have been playing in the snow without gloves or mittens

1. _____

2. _____

3. _____

4. _____

5. _____

6. _____

7. _____

8. _____

Part B

Now think of some other objects. Name the object and ask your partner to use an adjective from the domain to describe the temperature of that object.

Exercise 2: Word Puzzle

Using the definition given on the left, write the correct words or phrases from the HOT–COLD domain. When you finish, the letters in the boxes will spell the name of something used to measure temperature.

1. a lukewarm liquid   ☐ __ p __ __

2. like red-hot   __ __ i __ __ __ - ☐ o __

3. used for warm water   __ __ k ☐ __ __ m

4. means the same as "frosty"   __ ☐ __ g __

5. very hot and moist   __ t __ __ ☐ y __

6. so hot it could burn you   __ c ☐ __ __ __ i __ __

7. weather that is neither hot nor cold   w __ __ r ☐

8. below 32°F   __ __ r __ ☐ z __ __

9. the kind of weather Canada has in January   w __ __ ☐ r __

10. a very hot fire   __ ☐ d - __ __ t

11. as hot as fire   __ __ e ☐ __

A _____ is used to measure temperature.

Exercise 3: Word Choice

Part A

Choose a word from the domain that best completes the sentence and write it on the line.

1. If you pick up something that is __?__ , you will burn your hands.   1. _____

2. If you eat soup that is __?__ , you will burn your mouth.   2. _____

3. If your coffee is ? , you might think it is not hot enough.

3. _____

4. If your bedroom is ? , you might have to buy another blanket.

4. _____

5. If your hands are ? , you probably forgot to wear gloves.

5. _____

6. If the temperature in the classroom is ? , your teacher might cancel class.

6. _____

7. If you stay outside in the snow for two hours, your hands and feet might feel ? .

7. _____

8. If you visit Canada in January, be ready for temperatures that are ? .

8. _____

Part B

Now write four sentences of your own that are similar to those above. Leave a blank in each sentence so that your classmates can choose a word from the domain that completes the meaning of the sentence.

Exercise 4: For Discussion

Working with a partner, describe the temperature of your home town in summer, fall, winter and spring.

Exercise 5: For Discussion or Writing

Describe the hottest or coldest day you have ever experienced. Tell where you were, what you were doing, and how you felt.

V. Expanding the Domain

Verb and Noun Forms

Many of the adjectives in this domain also have verb or noun forms. Knowing the meaning of the verb or noun will help you understand and remember the meaning of the adjective.

Exercise 6: Dictionary Work

Part A

Look up the words below in a dictionary and write down their definitions.

1. to scorch _____

2. to sizzle _____

3. to steam _____

4. to scald _____

5. to chill _____

6. to freeze _____

7. a blister _____

8. a glacier _____

9. frost _____

Part B

Now complete the sentences below with a word from section A. Be sure to use the correct form of the word.

1. If you burn your skin badly, you might get a ⎯?⎯ .

1. _____

2. The meat ⎯?⎯ in the hot frying pan.

2. _____

3. There are many huge ⎯?⎯ in the mountains of Switzerland.

3. _____

4. If you don't move a hot iron quickly enough, you might ⎯?⎯ the fabric.

4. _____

5. Be careful when you drink hot liquids. You might ⎯?⎯ your tongue.

5. _____

6. On winter mornings, I like to look at the beautiful ⎯?⎯ on my bedroom window.

6. _____

VI. Expanding the Domain

Literal and Figurative Meanings

The words in the HOT–COLD domain aren't always used literally. They don't always refer to temperature. They can be used figuratively, as in the sentences below.

1. Federica gave the impolite clerk an icy stare.

In this sentence, icy has been used figuratively. A look can't be physically hot or cold, but it can be 'cold' in the sense of being unfriendly.

2. The teacher's scorching criticism of Andrew's work made him feel awful.

In this sentence, the word scorching means that the teacher's remarks were very negative.

Exercise 7: Literal or Figurative?

In the sentences below, some of the underlined words or expressions are used literally and others are used figuratively. Write *L* if the meaning is *literal* and *F* if it is *figurative*.

_____ 1. The new students from Thailand were pleased by the warm welcome they received from the president of the university.

_____ 2. Don't go outside. It's scorching today.

_____ 3. Paul has a red-hot idea that he wants to tell his boss about. He thinks it's such a good idea that he'll get a promotion.

_____ 4. As the Berlin Wall came down, people all over the world knew that the cold war between the Soviet Union and the U.S. was ending.

_____ 5. When I come in from the snow, I like to drink a cup of piping hot tea.

_____ 6. Ernesto's new car is hot. It can go from 0 to 60 mph in 10 seconds.

_____ 7. It's chilly in here. Is the furnace broken?

_____ 8. The Prime Minister made a blistering attack on the proposed law. It was obvious that he strongly opposed it.

_____ 9. Karl has a fiery temper. He gets angry quickly and easily, which sometimes gets him in trouble.

_____ 10. Enrica got a frosty reception at her boyfriend's house. She thinks his parents don't like her.

Exercise 8: For Discussion

Work with a partner or in a small group. Discuss the meanings of the expressions below. Be ready to tell the class what you think each expression means.

1. (a) a warm personality
   (b) a hot-tempered person

2. (a) a lukewarm response
   (b) a blistering response

UNIT 12

How's the Weather?

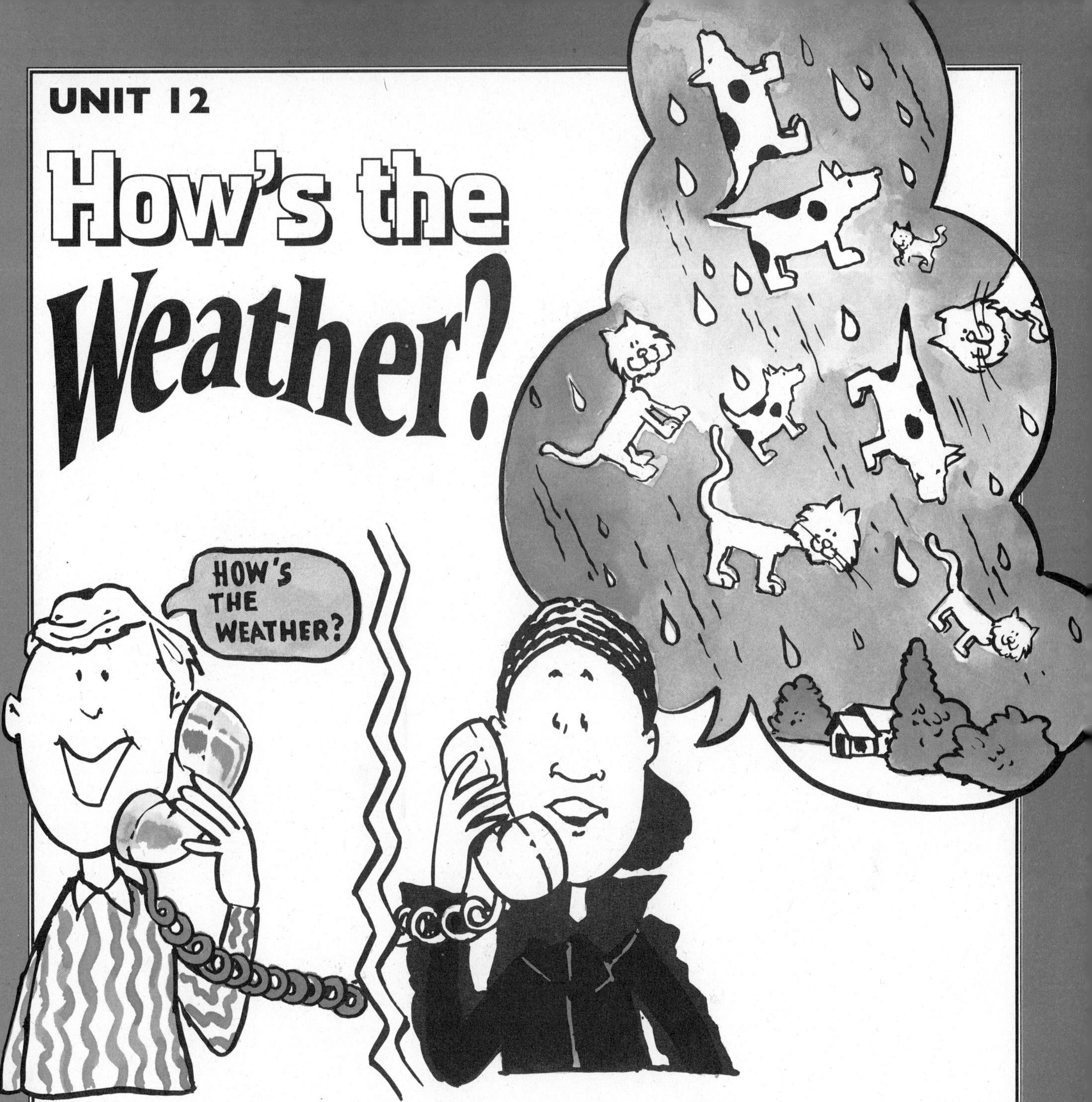

THE WEATHER DOMAIN

I. Getting Ready

An Englishman once said that everybody talks about the weather, but nobody does anything about it. The weather is certainly a common topic of conversation. When you are chatting with someone you don't know well, the weather is always a safe topic. You can even ask a stranger the question, "How's the weather?"

Discuss the following questions with your whole class or in a small group.

1. Do you listen to the radio in the morning to learn what the weather for the day will be? Why?
2. How do you feel when it rains?
3. What's your favorite kind of weather? Do you like it warm and sunny, cool and windy, or cold and snowy?

II. Introducing the Domain

There are many words in English for talking about the weather. Some give information about the humidity, the amount of moisture in the air. Others tell us about rain and other forms of precipitation, the moisture falling out of the sky. Still other words are used for different kinds of winds and storms. Some nouns and adjectives in the WEATHER domain are presented below. Look over the chart and mark any words that you don't know.

The WEATHER Domain

Precipitation (Falling Moisture)

Not Frozen

mist
drizzle
sprinkle
shower
rain
downpour

A unit of rain: raindrop

Frozen

snow
snow flurry
snowfall

freezing rain
sleet
hail

A unit of snow: snowflake

Reduced Visibility (Visible Moisture or Particles in Air)

mist
haze
fog
smog

Storms

rainstorm
thunderstorm
  thunder
  lightning
snowstorm
blizzard
windstorm

Adjectives for Humidity (Amount of Moisture in Air)

Low

dry
arid

High

humid
muggy
steamy

Wind (Moving Air)

breeze
wind
gale

A unit of wind: gust of wind

III. Exploring the Domain

The WEATHER Domain

A. Sometimes it rains so lightly that you don't need an umbrella. We call a fine rain like this a mist. A drizzle or a sprinkle is also a light rain. There are just a few raindrops coming down. If the rain is heavier, but doesn't last very long, we might call it a shower. The heaviest kind of rainfall of all is a downpour.

mist	rain
drizzle	downpour
sprinkle	raindrop
shower	

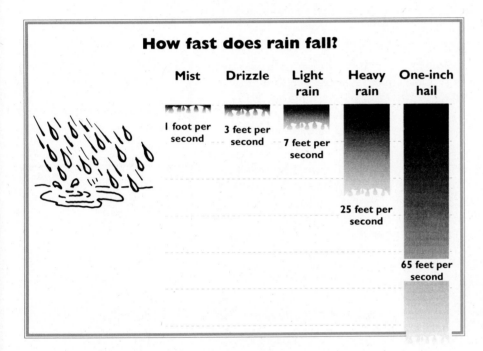

How fast does rain fall?

Mist	Drizzle	Light rain	Heavy rain	One-inch hail
1 foot per second	3 feet per second	7 feet per second	25 feet per second	65 feet per second

Different kinds of precipitation fall at different speeds because of different air resistance—not because of their different weights.

B. When the weather forecast calls for light snow flurries, most people don't care. It's only a few snowflakes in the air. But if a heavy snowfall is predicted, some people get very worried.

snow	snowfall
snow flurry	snowflake

C. Moisture falling from the sky isn't always rain or snow. If the temperature is near freezing (32°F or 0°C) this moisture might be sleet, a combination of freezing rain and melting snow. When rain falls through freezing air, it may freeze as it hits the ground. This form of precipitation is known as freezing rain. The rain freezes on everything it touches–trees, cars, and roads. Hail is frozen raindrops or small balls of ice. Hail can come at any time of year.

freezing rain
sleet
hail

D. On a very hot day a breeze or light wind is welcome. The moving air helps us feel cooler. Small, sudden gusts of wind are also refreshing, though they might blow your hat off! A gale, a powerful wind, can cause serious damage. Gale-force winds can rip the roofs off buildings and knock over large trees.

breeze	gale
wind	gust of wind

E. Storm is the word we use for violent or severe weather. A storm with lots of rain is a rainstorm. When there are loud claps of thunder and bright flashes of lightning, it is called a thunderstorm. A storm with lots of snow is a snowstorm. An especially severe snowstorm with very high wind and blinding snow is a blizzard. We have windstorms as well, when there is a very strong wind but no precipitation.

storm
rainstorm
thunderstorm
lightning
thunder
snowstorm
blizzard
windstorm

F. In the Sahara Desert the temperature is very high during the day and the air is very dry. This is a hot, arid climate. Because the humidity is low, we don't mind the scorching heat so much. Washington, D.C., on the other hand, can be steamy. On many blistering summer days the humidity is very high. No one wants to be outside in this hot, muggy weather.

dry	humid
arid	muggy
	steamy

G. Occasionally you can see the moisture in the air. In the morning there is sometimes a slight mist or haze which goes away in the heat of the day. A mist doesn't cause serious problems with visibility (seeing into the distance), but fog often does. Being in fog is like being in a cloud. Visibility is also reduced by smog, a combination of smoke and fog. It lasts longer than fog and is very unpleasant. Smog is a man-made problem, caused by pollution from cars or factories. Smog is a serious problem in large cities such as Los Angeles, London, and Tokyo.

mist
haze
fog
smog

IV. Exercises

The WEATHER Domain

Exercise 1: Beginning Practice

Study the WEATHER domain for a few minutes and then place the words below in the correct columns. Do this as quickly as you can. Then check your answers.

breeze	blizzard	rain
fog	sprinkle	sleet
snow flurry	mist	humid
shower	smog	freezing rain
lightning	drizzle	thunder
haze	dry	muggy
gust	hail	wind
downpour	gale	snow
arid	steamy	rainstorm

Precipitation (Falling Moisture) *Not Frozen*	Reduced Visibility (Visible Moisture or Particles in Air)	Adjectives for Humidity (Amount of Moisture in Air) *Low*
_____	_____	_____
_____	_____	_____
_____	_____	*High*
_____		_____
_____		_____
Frozen	Storms	Wind (Moving Air)
_____	_____	_____
_____	_____	_____
_____	_____	_____
_____	_____	_____

Exercise 2: Matching

Part A

Match the descriptions with a WEATHER word. Write the correct word on the line.

muggy	breeze	shower
haze	flurry	sleet

1. light snow   1. _____

2. brief rainfall   2. _____

3. particles in the air that reduce visibility   3. _____

4. light wind   4. _____

5. describes warm, wet air   5. _____

6. partly frozen rain   6. _____

Part B

Now match these descriptions and WEATHER words.

drizzle   blizzard
downpour   gale
fog   hail

1. a strong wind   1. _____

2. small lumps of ice   2. _____

3. a severe snowstorm with a lot of wind   3. _____

4. very heavy rain   4. _____

5. moisture so thick you can see it   5. _____

6. light rain   6. _____

Exercise 3: Sentence Completion

Some nouns for weather also have a verb form. If you don't know the verbs which go with the following nouns, look them up in a dictionary. Then complete the sentences with the correct form of the verb.

1. We couldn't go to the park yesterday because it was (*rain*) __?__ .   1. _____

2. We don't really need an umbrella today. It is only (*drizzle*) __?__ .   2. _____

3. We had a terrible snowstorm last January. It (*snow*) __?__ for two whole days.   3. _____

4. It was a beautiful clear day, but suddenly a wind came up and the sky (*cloud*) __?__ over.   4. _____

Exercise 4: Sentence Completion

Many nouns for weather also have an adjective form. If you don't know the adjectives which go with the nouns listed below, look them up in a dictionary. Then complete the sentences with the adjective.

1. The state of Oregon in the United States is known for its (*rain*) __?__ weather.   1. _____

2. Because we live near the ocean, we often have cool, (*mist*) __?__ mornings.   2. _____

3. Two days after the blizzard, we all went for a walk through the (*snow*) __?__ streets of town.   3. _____

4. We decided not to drive to Boston last weekend because the roads were too (*ice*) __?__ .   4. _____

5. When I looked out the window, I could see it was a beautiful, (*sun*) __?__ day.   5. _____

6. Cornwall is a part of England that sticks out into the ocean. It is almost always (*wind*) __?__ there.

6. _____

7. We drove very slowly because it was a dark, (*fog*) __?__ night. We couldn't see more than two feet in front of us.

7. _____

8. The weather forecast predicted partly (*cloud*) __?__ skies for this afternoon.

8. _____

What have you learned about forming adjectives from nouns for weather?

_____

Exercise 5: Sense or Nonsense?

Decide whether each of the following sentences makes sense or is nonsense. Then circle the correct word.

1. We went to the desert on our vacation because we love muggy weather.	SENSE	NONSENSE
2. The forecast is for freezing rain. It will be a good night for driving.	SENSE	NONSENSE
3. Key West, Florida, has a very pleasant climate. Even when it's hot, there's usually a light breeze.	SENSE	NONSENSE
4. My friend Yuki lives in the city. There's a lot of smog there so she always carries an umbrella.	SENSE	NONSENSE
5. We haven't had much rain here this summer and the farmers are hoping for hail.	SENSE	NONSENSE
6. The picnic was ruined when we got caught in a sudden downpour.	SENSE	NONSENSE
7. They had to close the airport because of very heavy fog.	SENSE	NONSENSE
8. We like living here because the temperatures are blistering in summer and the air is very humid.	SENSE	NONSENSE
9. My little sister loves to play outside when it is drizzling.	SENSE	NONSENSE
10. It's fun to play in a blizzard.	SENSE	NONSENSE
11. The most frightening thing about the thunderstorm last night was the gale-force winds.	SENSE	NONSENSE

Exercise 6: For Discussion or Writing

What do you like about the weather where you are living now? What don't you like?

Exercise 7: For Discussion or Writing

What would you do if you had to travel to a city or country you don't know anything about? How would you know what kind of weather to expect? You might look in a book like *The Times Books World Weather Guide*. This book gives information about the weather in many cities of the world.

The chart below has been adapted from this book. It gives information about temperature and precipitation for four cities in the world.

City	Month	Temperature °F Average Daily		Temperature °C Average Daily		Precipitation Average Number of Days
		Max	Min	Max	Min	
Hyderabad, India	Jan.	84	60	29	16	0.5
	July	87	73	31	23	11
Mossamedes, Angola	Jan.	79	65	26	18	1
	July	68	56	20	13	0
Norman Wells, Canada	Jan.	−11	−26	−24	−32	14
	July	72	50	22	10	10
Paris, France	Jan.	43	34	6	1	17
	July	76	58	25	15	12

Part A

Answer the following questions.

1. How many days can you expect it to rain in Paris in the month of January?

2. In January in Norman Wells there is a lot of precipitation. What kind of precipitation do you think it is?

3. Will you need to take a coat to Mossamedes in July? Will you need an umbrella?

4. In what city is it hotter in January than in July?

5. Which city has the most rainfall?

Part B

With your class or in a small group, answer the questions below. Explain your answers using words from the WEATHER domain and the HOT–COLD domain.

1. You have to go to Paris in January. What clothing should you bring along?

2. You have a two-week vacation in July. Where would you like to go? Why?

3. Would you like to live in Norman Wells, Canada? Why or why not?

4. Which of the cities listed here would you like to live in? Why?

Exercise 8: Reading

Last summer Manuel spent a week in the mountains. He kept a daily record, or diary, of his trip. He recorded a lot of information about the weather. Reading parts of his diary will help you better understand the words in this domain. As you read, underline any words you find from the WEATHER domain.

A Week in the Mountains

Saturday. We left Los Angeles. The city was covered with smog as usual and we were looking forward to a week of clean, clear air. We headed east up into the Angeles Mountains.

The drive up into the mountains was gorgeous. As we climbed higher and higher, the air became cool and crisp. We stopped for a break and in the distance we could see the outline of the next mountain, covered with haze. The peak was hidden in a cloud.

The drive to the top wasn't very pleasant, however. As we neared the peak we found that the fog had thickened. Because of the dense, thick fog we couldn't see in front of us and we could only travel a few miles an hour. We put up our tents at a campsite near the top.

Sunday. We woke up early. There was a wonderful view from our camp. The fog had lifted and there was only a slight mist as we looked out over the countryside. We spent a wonderful day exploring the mountain.

Tuesday. An official of the campsite came by this afternoon to warn us of a snowstorm. She said that heavy snowfall was expected and that if the wind became worse, it could turn into a blizzard. They were asking everyone to leave. We were disappointed, but packed up our camp and headed back down the mountain.

The official was right, too. As we were loading the car, it began to snow. At first there were just flurries but the snow was falling steadily as we left the peak. We watched the snowflakes land on our windshield and were sorry we couldn't stay to enjoy the snow. We headed north to a different park in the valley.

Thursday. We woke up to another beautiful day – clear blue skies and a light breeze. We decided to hike to a nearby lake and have lunch. The walk to the lake was very pleasant. The path went through a forest and there was a light mist in the air. By noon it was quite hot. We were all exhausted by the time we reached the lake.

We spread a blanket out on the grass for a picnic lunch. But suddenly we noticed a change in the weather. Some clouds rolled in and it began to sprinkle. The sun was still shining, though, and we continued to eat in the light drizzle. We didn't mind getting a little wet. In fact, after the long hike through the woods, the shower was very refreshing.

But soon the clouds began to darken and there were big gusts of wind. It was clear that a thunderstorm was coming. We knew it was dangerous to be outside in thunder and lightning and began to look for shelter. Fortunately, we spotted an old, dilapidated cabin by the edge of the lake and raced to it just as the storm broke. The thunder was terrible and the lightning struck a 45 nearby tree. What a downpour! I've never seen such rain!

The storm was over as suddenly as it began. The skies cleared and we returned safely to our camp.

Sunday. Our last day of vacation turned out to be very windy. The afternoon sky was dark and cloudy. It seemed to be turning colder. As we left the camp- 50 site, we heard that the forecast was for several days of rain and fog. We were glad to be going home.

Exercise 9: For Writing

Keep your own weather diary for a week. Share your diary with the class or in a small group.

V. Introducing a Related Domain

The NATURAL DISASTERS Domain

Rain, fog, and snow are everyday events. They may upset our plans, but we usually don't pay very much attention to them. The words in the next domain describe natural disasters like floods and hurricanes. They are much more serious.

Have you ever experienced a natural disaster? If so, your teacher may ask you to share your experience with the class.

Words in the NATURAL DISASTERS domain are given in the chart below. Look over the chart and mark any words that you don't know.

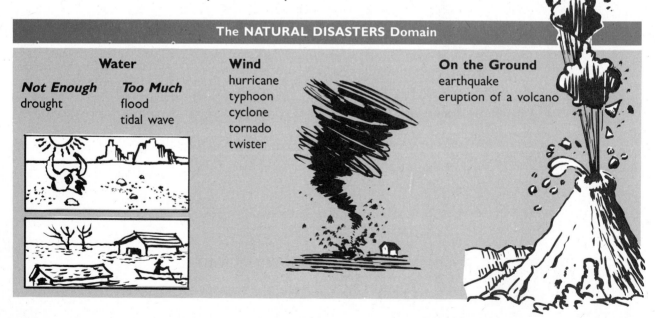

The NATURAL DISASTERS Domain

Water		Wind	On the Ground
Not Enough	*Too Much*	hurricane	earthquake
drought	flood	typhoon	eruption of a volcano
	tidal wave	cyclone	
		tornado	
		twister	

VI. Exploring the Domain

A. *Not enough water.* Plants and animals need water to survive. That is why a long period without rain, called a drought, is so terrible. During a drought, plants dry up and die. If the drought continues, it leads to famine, a shortage of food.

| drought |

B. *Too much water.* Heavy rain brings a lot of water. It can cause a river to rise above its banks and overflow onto the surrounding land. This is called a flood. Floods can be terribly destructive, causing damage to houses and other property. A tidal wave is a large ocean wave that floods inland from the shore.

| flood
tidal wave |

C. Hurricanes and typhoons are severe tropical storms that have high winds and heavy rain. Typically they cover a large area (310 miles or 500 kilometers in diameter) and have spiraling winds of more than 70 miles per hour (31.3 meters per second). The difference between hurricanes and typhoons depends only on where they are. Severe tropical storms in the western Pacific Ocean are called typhoons. The same type of storm is called a hurricane in the Caribbean and the United States. (Some people also call such storms cyclones, particularly if they occur in the Indian Ocean.)

| hurricane
typhoon
cyclone |

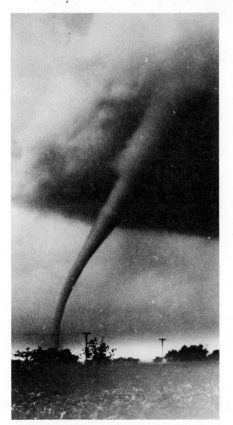

D. Although the damage caused by a hurricane is great, its intensity does not equal that of a tornado. Like a hurricane, a tornado, or twister, consists of spiraling winds, which are rotating very rapidly. Unlike a hurricane, a tornado cloud, a dark circular funnel, covers a relatively small area (55–550 yards or 50–500 meters) and its force is very concentrated. If it touches the ground, it can completely level buildings which are in its path.

| tornado
twister |

E. The last two words in the NATURAL DISASTERS domain do not describe weather, but they are important natural disasters which affect everyone. An earthquake is a sudden and violent shaking of the earth, caused by changes in the earth's crust. In 1985 there was a terrible earthquake in

| earthquake
volcano |

Mexico City, in which many buildings in the center of the city were destroyed and thousands of people died.

A volcano creates a mountain with a large opening in the top. If the volcano erupts, or explodes, hot molten (melted) rock, known as lava, pours out.

VII. Exercises

Exercise 10: Crossword Puzzle

Complete the crossword puzzle below using words from the NATURAL DISASTERS domain.

Down:

1. a dark, funnel-shaped cloud
2. a storm with high winds and rain, in the Pacific
3. a shortage of rain
5. a sudden shaking of the surface of the earth

Across

4. a river overflows its banks
6. a tropical storm in the Caribbean
7. an exploding mountain
8. another word for tornado

Exercise 11: For Writing or Discussion

Describe a natural disaster that occurred in your country. If you don't know of any natural disaster, talk to other students or check in an encyclopedia.

VIII. Expanding the Domain

Figurative Meanings

We don't always use words in the WEATHER domain literally. We don't always use them to talk about the weather. Sometimes they are used in other contexts as well. For example, the word breeze in the following sentence is not being used literally.

That quiz was a breeze.

In this sentence breeze doesn't mean "wind." If a quiz is a breeze, that means it is very easy.

Exercise 12: Literal or Figurative?

Read each sentence below and decide if the underlined WEATHER word is being used literally, to talk about the weather, or if it is being used figuratively, in some other sense. Write *L* (*literal*) or *F* (*figurative*). Your teacher may ask you to discuss the meanings of the figurative uses of these words from the WEATHER domain.

_____ 1. I like Juanita so much because she is so friendly and is always smiling. She has such a sunny disposition.

_____ 2. We heard on the news that there was a terrible windstorm in the Gobi Desert.

_____ 3. My father and his friends from college get together once a month and talk about the good old days. They like to play cards and shoot the breeze.

_____ 4. *Celia:* What are you going to do during summer vacation?

Denise: I haven't the foggiest idea.

_____ 5. Mr. and Mrs. Wang were very uncomfortable sightseeing in Charleston, South Carolina, because it was so muggy there.

_____ 6. The boss told Stan he was fired. Then Stan stormed angrily out of the room.

_____ 7. My grandmother had beautiful snow-white hair.

_____ **8.** My sister is getting married and we are going to have a wedding <u>shower</u> for her next week. All our friends and relatives will be there. I'm sure she will get many beautiful gifts.

_____ **9.** We got caught in a <u>thunderstorm</u> and my dress was ruined!

_____ **10.** Yuriko was reading *Love Story,* a popular romance with a sad ending. When she finished the last chapter and put the book down, her eyes were <u>misty</u>.

_____ **11.** I drove into Tokyo and was going to stay there for a week. The <u>smog</u> was so bad that my eyes hurt and I began to cough. I decided to leave before breakfast.

_____ **12.** Jamal earned quite a bit of money this summer, but he's not going to spend it. He's saving it for a <u>rainy</u> day.

Exercise 13: For Discussion

In many areas of the world there are special kinds of wind. In the Alps, in Europe, for example, a <u>foehn</u> is a warm, dry wind which blows down from the mountains. Are there special kinds of wind in your native country? What are they called?

Exercise 14: For Discussion

In English there are a number of informal expressions for very heavy rain. Have you ever heard these expressions?

    It's raining cats and dogs.
    It's raining buckets.
    It's raining pitchforks and hammer handles.

What are some informal expressions in your native language for heavy rain?

The Best of Times
and
The Worst of Times

THE BEST—WORST DOMAIN

I. Getting Ready

We constantly evaluate things in our lives. We are always asking each other about movies, new products, or even other people. "Is that new movie any good?" "What do you think of your biology class?"

Just as we evaluate the world and people around us, we are evaluated by others: parents, employers, and teachers. Teachers tell us if we are good students or not. Usually, they base their evaluations on our tests, homework, and other assignments.

In the United States, most teachers give students letter grades of A, B, C, D, or F. The chart below shows what these grades usually stand for.

Grading Scale				
Very Good	**Good**	**Average**	**Bad**	**Very Bad**
A	B	C	D	F
90–100%	80–89%	70–79%	60–69%	0–59%

Discuss the following questions with your whole class or in a small group. Be honest!

1. What is the best grade to get on a test? What is the worst grade?
2. In what class(es) did you get the best grades in school?

II. Introducing the Domain

A student who gets A's on all her assignments and tests is an <u>excellent</u> student. Her work is <u>superior</u>. She probably studies very hard. Teachers think it's <u>wonderful</u> to have such <u>outstanding</u> students.

A student who doesn't ever study and who misses class a lot is a <u>terrible</u> student. That student will probably get D's or even F's. These are <u>awful</u> grades. Teachers are often concerned about students who get such <u>appalling</u> grades.

These two students represent two extremes, the best and the worst of students. There are many words in English that talk about the best and the worst. The BEST–WORST domain is given on page 123. Look over the words in the chart and mark any words you don't know.

III. Exercises

Exercise 1: Beginning Practice

Study the BEST–WORST domain carefully for a few minutes. Then look at the words following the chart and write *B* (*the Best*) or *W* (*the Worst*). Do this exercise as quickly as you can. Then check your answers by looking at the domain.

The Best
the best
excellent
exceptional
extraordinary
fabulous
fantastic
first-class
first-rate
grand
great
magnificent
marvelous
outstanding
perfect
sensational
spectacular
splendid
superb
superior
terrific
topnotch
wonderful

■ *Informal*
awesome
out-of-this-world
super

The Worst
the worst
terrible
horrible
dreadful
awful

appalling
atrocious
wretched
abominable
horrendous

■ *Informal*
lousy
no good
rotten
low-down

_____ 1. no good

_____ 2. wonderful

_____ 3. marvelous

_____ 4. terrific

_____ 5. awesome

_____ 6. rotten

_____ 7. extraordinary

_____ 8. lousy

_____ 9. wretched

_____ 10. topnotch

_____ 11. abominable

_____ 12. horrendous

_____ 13. fantastic

_____ 14. outstanding

_____ 15. appalling

_____ 16. splendid

_____ 17. out-of-this-world

_____ 18. low-down

_____ 19. superb

_____ 20. atrocious

Exercise 2: Sentence Completion

Read each group of sentences and then choose the better word or phrase and write it on the line.

1. Mr. Hulot took a vacation at the beach. It rained the whole time he was there. He decided to do some reading, but he forgot to bring his books with him. He had __?__ vacation. (*an exceptional, a dreadful*)

2. Somebody ran into Shoko's car. She immediately took it to her car dealer. It was repaired and looked as good as new in two days. She recommended the dealer to her friends because the company had done such __?__ repair job on her car. (*a fantastic, an atrocious*)

3. Karen wanted to invite her boyfriend to see a new movie. But he said that he had already seen it and it wasn't very good. In fact, he thought it was __?__ . (*terrific, terrible*)

4. There are still many beautiful forests in the world, but these __?__ places are rapidly being destroyed by man-made pollution. (*magnificent, appalling*)

5. On Independence Day, Washington, D.C. has one of the largest fireworks shows in the United States. This city is __?__ place to visit on July 4th. (*a marvelous, an awful*)

6. Davis, California, has the largest number of bicycles per capita in the United States. The area is relatively flat so bicycling is a __?__ way of getting around. (*perfect, rotten*)

7. Carla used to be one of my best friends, but one day she started telling lies about me. It was a really __?__ thing for her to do. (*fabulous, lousy*)

8. Woo-Jin was making tea. He forgot to turn off the stove when he left the house for an hour. When he came back, the smell of smoke filled the house. Fortunately, the house didn't burn down, but the smell was really __?__ and lasted for about a week. (*first-rate, horrible*)

1. _____

2. _____

3. _____

4. _____

5. _____

6. _____

7. _____

8. _____

Exercise 3: Word Choice

Look at the cartoon on the next page. The three boys are talking about what the perfect world might be like. They use the word perfect over and over again. When writing in English, it is usually better to use different words and not to repeat the same one many times.

Choose a word from the domain to complete the following sentences and write it on the line.

1. In the perfect world, everything would be __?__ .

2. The perfect world would have __?__ weather.

3. The perfect world would have __?__ food.

4. In the perfect world, everyone would look __?__ .

5. In such a __?__ world, it would be hard to know what "perfect" was!

1. _____

2. _____

3. _____

4. _____

5. _____

For Better or For Worse®   by Lynn Johnston

FOR BETTER OR FOR WORSE COPYRIGHT 1990 Lynn Johnston. Reprinted with permission of Universal Press Syndicate.

Exercise 4: Sentence Completion

Complete five of these sentences. (Choose the five that are the most interesting to you.) Discuss your answers with your group or the whole class.

1. A <u>magnificent</u> place to visit in my city or country is

   _____

   _____ .

2. I get a <u>horrendous</u> headache whenever

   _____ .

3. The _____ is a car that gives a <u>topnotch</u> performance.

4. _____ is a good place for <u>sensational</u> bargains.

5. One of the most <u>extraordinary</u> recent events in the world

   was _____

   _____ .

6. What <u>atrocious</u> behavior! Did you see what that little boy

   did? He _____ .

7. "_____" is a <u>horrible</u> movie

   because _____ .

Exercise 5: Sense or Nonsense?

Decide whether each of the sentences below makes sense or is nonsense. Then circle the correct word.

1. After she gave an <u>atrocious</u> speech, she received a standing ovation.   SENSE   NONSENSE

2. That guy writes a best seller every year. He's a <u>first-class</u> writer.   SENSE   NONSENSE

3. A hovel is a <u>superior</u> place to live.   SENSE   NONSENSE

4. There was plenty of good food and interesting conversation at the party. We had a <u>fabulous</u> time.   SENSE   NONSENSE

5. Charles Dickens was a <u>dreadful</u> writer of the 19th century.   SENSE   NONSENSE

6. They served us burned chicken at "Chez Nous." It was a <u>marvelous</u> meal.   SENSE   NONSENSE

7. The sun is shining and the birds are singing. What a <u>spectacular</u> day!   SENSE   NONSENSE

8. I paid $10.95 for that plastic ballpoint pen. It was an <u>exceptional</u> bargain.   SENSE   NONSENSE

9. I really don't like my neighbor at all. His behavior is <u>appalling</u>.   SENSE   NONSENSE

10. The actress was so believable and genuine in her role of the widowed mother. She gave an <u>outstanding</u> performance.   SENSE   NONSENSE

Exercise 6: Word Choice

In the United States some magazines publish reviews of "The Best" and "The Worst" attractions in the area such as restaurants, bakeries, movie theaters, and parks.

Below is an example of such a review. All the words that show whether it is good or bad have been taken out. Imagine that you have visited this bakery. Complete the sentences with words from the BEST–WORST domain to show how you feel about this bagel bakery.

One of _____ bagel bakeries in the Seattle area is

Bright's Bagel Bakery. Their bagels are _____ and they

also carry other _____ baked goods, such as a/an

_____ blueberry muffin and a/an

_____ fudge brownie.

Exercise 7: For Writing

Write your own short review (3–5 sentences) of a local attraction in your country or in the United States. Share your review with other students in the class.

Exercise 8: Sentence Writing

You probably have a lot of information about the United States, especially if you are living in the U.S. now. You have your own ideas and opinions about what its strengths and weaknesses are.

What do you think about the United States? How would you evaluate it? What are the best things about it? What are the worst things?

With a partner or by yourself, write ten sentences that describe the strengths and weaknesses that you have observed in the United States. In your sentences, use some of the adjectives from the BEST–WORST domain. (If you are not familiar with the U.S., you can write sentences about your own country or some other country that you know well.)

Exercise 9: For Discussion and Writing

What would your perfect world look like or be like? Discuss this question with your whole class or in a small group. Then take 10 or 15 minutes to write a description of your perfect world.

IV. Expanding the Domain

> More about the BEST—WORST Domain

Exercise 10: For Discussion

In this chapter we have presented only some of the words in the BEST–WORST domain. You can find many other adjectives of evaluation which belong in this domain, especially if you listen to informal, conversational English. People are constantly creating new ways to say that something is the best or the worst.

Ask your teacher or an American about some current slang expressions for the best and the worst. Discuss them with your classmates.

Exercise 11: Sentence Completion

Many of the adjectives in this domain have related adverbs which end in *-ly*. Read each sentence and decide whether an adjective or an adverb should be used. Write the correct word on the line.

Ronald Reagan was not an __(1)__ (*exceptional, exceptionally*) famous actor. However, many Americans think he was a __(2)__ (*great, greatly*) president. He was an __(3)__ (*excellent, excellently*) communicator. At press conferences, he performed __(4)__ (*superb, superbly*).

    Reagan acted in cowboy movies. Cowboy movies were __(5)__ (*outstanding, outstandingly*) popular in the 1940s and 1950s. One of the most famous actors in cowboy movies was John Wayne. He had a __(6)__ (*magnificent, magnificently*) career as a cowboy star.

    The cowboy movies of John Wayne, Ronald Reagan, and other western actors, often created __(7)__ (*dreadful, dreadfully*) myths or untruths about what really happened in the "Old West." In these cowboy movies, Native Americans

1. _____

2. _____

3. _____

4. _____

5. _____

6. _____

7. _____

were frequently portrayed as a __(8)__ (*terrible, terribly*) group of people. In these movies, the Native Americans sometimes had __(9)__ (*horrendous, horrendously*) scary faces, and the white settlers looked __(10)__ (*terrible, terribly*) frightened. Because of these negative images of Native Americans in movies, many people thought the Native Americans __(11)__ were (*horrible, horribly*).

However, in reality, the record shows that it was the Native Americans who were treated __(12)__ (*wretched, wretchedly*) by white settlers and government agents. Even today, in some communities, Native Americans and other minorities are treated with __(13)__ (*appalling, appallingly*) disrespect.

8. _____

9. _____

10. _____

11. _____

12. _____

13. _____

Exercise 12: For Discussion and Writing

Part A

Advertisers often use adjectives to describe their products. The advertisement on the next page uses many adjectives from the BEST–WORST domain.

Discuss the following questions:

1. How many words for <u>best</u> can you find in this advertisement?

2. Are there any words in the advertisement that are not in the BEST–WORST domain on page 123?

3. Why do you think this advertisement was put in the newspaper? What is the purpose of the ad?

YOU'RE NUMBER ONE
STUPENDOUS
FIRST CLASS
FIRST RATE
TREMENDOUS
UNBEATABLE
WONDERFUL
GREAT
TOP BANANA
WOW! THE BEST
MAGNIFICENT
TOPS NONE BETTER SUPER

When it comes to our employees,
we're never at a loss for words.

FAIRFAX HOSPITAL
INOVA FAIRFAX HOSPITAL SYSTEM

Part B

Find an example of an advertisement from a magazine or newspaper *or* write a description of a commercial from TV that uses words from the BEST–WORST domain.

Part C

Write your own short ad for a real or imaginary product. Use some words from the BEST–WORST domain.

Exercise 13: For Discussion

The title of this unit is "The Best of Times and the Worst of Times." It is the beginning of a very famous book, *A Tale of Two Cities,* by Charles Dickens. The first paragraph of the book is given below.

> It was the best of times, it was the worst of times, it was the age of wisdom, it was the age of foolishness, it was the epoch of belief, it was the epoch of incredulity, it was the season of Light, it was the season of Darkness, it was the spring of hope, it was the winter of despair, we had everything before us, we had nothing before us, we were all going direct to Heaven, we were all going direct the other way.

In this passage find as many pairs of opposites (like best/worst) as you can. Do you agree with Dickens that they represent some of the best and the worst parts of life?

I. Getting Ready

The TEACH and LEARN Domains

We start learning from the moment we are born. We learn things from our parents, our teachers, and our friends. We also learn from our experiences.

Discuss the following questions with your whole class or in a small group.

1. What is one of the most important things that you have learned from your parents?
2. How do you prefer to learn? Do you like to watch someone do something, have someone tell you how to do it, or try to do it yourself?
3. What is (was) your favorite class in high school? What did the teacher do to teach you?

II. Introducing the Domain

The TEACH Domain

Teaching involves the giving or sharing of information so that others may learn it. The following chart shows some words we use in English to describe different kinds of teaching.

Look over the domain and mark the words that you don't know.

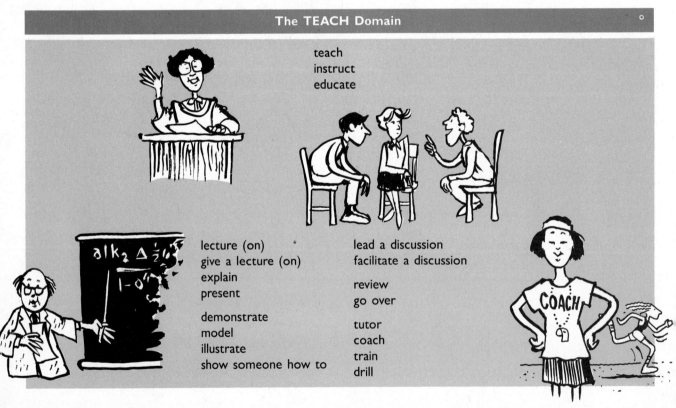

The TEACH Domain

teach
instruct
educate

lecture (on)
give a lecture (on)
explain
present

demonstrate
model
illustrate
show someone how to

lead a discussion
facilitate a discussion

review
go over

tutor
coach
train
drill

III. Exploring the Domain

The countries of the world have many different ways of educating students. Let's look for a moment at an American high school. As you read, think about whether high school classes in your country are similar or different.

A Look at Newton High School

Newton High School is a typical American high school. If you could wander through the halls of this school one day and look into different classrooms, this is what you might see:

A. In a tenth grade history class, Ms. Hollister is <u>giving a lecture</u> on the American Civil War. She is <u>explaining</u> how and why the war started. While she is <u>lecturing</u>, most of the students are taking notes because Ms. Hollister is <u>presenting</u> this information to them for the first time.

> lecture (on) explain
> give a lecture present
> (on)

B. In the next room, Mr. Lee's chemistry class is doing something quite different. Mr. Lee is <u>showing</u> the students <u>how to</u> use a Bunsen burner correctly. He is <u>modeling</u> the method that he wants the students to use for heating a flask of water. While he is <u>demonstrating</u> this, a few students at the table in the back are miserable. They're freezing and would like to use the scalding hot water to make some hot chocolate!

> demonstrate
> model
> illustrate
> show someone how to

In another class across the hall, the art teacher is <u>illustrating</u> the effects of mixing various oil colors. He then <u>demonstrates</u> how adding infinitesimal amounts of white paint changes the quality of the color.

C. The three classes you have just visited are fairly quiet. But in Mr. Armstrong's sociology class, everybody is talking. He is <u>leading a discussion</u> on cultural diversity and everybody has something to say. He is making sure that everybody gets a chance to talk. Soon he is going to divide the class into smaller groups. While these groups are working on their assignment, Mr. Armstrong will go around the room and listen to each group and help them if they need it. He will try to <u>facilitate their discussions</u> without interfering too much.

> lead a discussion
> facilitate a discussion

D. One of the students in Mr. Armstrong's class is having trouble focusing on the discussion. She is worried about the test the class is going to have the next day. She wants the discussion to be over because she knows that Mr. Armstrong is going to <u>review</u> for the test. He will <u>go over</u> all the material that the students have studied this week.

> review
> go over

E. Let's take a quick look at what else is happening at the school. Ms. Harada, a volunteer, is helping one of the students with reading. She is tutoring the student on how to recognize and sound out certain words. In the gym, on the other side of the campus, Ms. Wright is coaching the girls' basketball team. Right now, she is training them to shoot baskets. They practice again and again, as she drills them on shooting techniques. The girls are standing in line and one after the other they try to shoot a basket. Ms. Wright believes that "practice makes perfect!"

> tutor
> coach
> train
> drill

F. In front of Newton High School, a car full of students has just pulled into the parking lot. They are taking the driver's education course. One of the students is driving while Mr. Diaz is sitting in the passenger's seat. Mr. Diaz has just spent the past hour instructing the students in how to make right and left turns. The day after tomorrow, a police officer is going to come to the class to educate the students about the dangers of drinking and driving. The police officer thinks it's very important to teach young people to be careful drivers.

> teach
> instruct
> educate

IV. Exercises

The TEACH Domain

Exercise 1: Sentence Completion

Choose the word from the domain that best describes what each person at Newton High School was doing and write it on the line.

1. Mr. Armstrong was __?__ a discussion. (*demonstrating, leading, instructing*)

   1. _____

2. One student was not concentrating. She was thinking about the test the next day. She wanted the teacher to __?__ the material for the test. (*tutor, educate, review*)

   2. _____

3. Ms. Hollister was __?__ the origins of the Civil War. (*modeling, lecturing on, training*)

   3. _____

4. Mr. Lee was __?__ how to use a Bunsen burner to heat water. (*leading, facilitating, demonstrating*)

   4. _____

5. Ms. Harada was __?__ one student in reading. (*presenting, going over, tutoring*)

   5. _____

6. Ms. Wright was __?__ the girls to shoot baskets. (*training, illustrating, explaining*)

   6. _____

7. A police officer came to __?__ the students about the dangers of drinking and driving. (*demonstrate, educate, explain*)

   7. _____

Exercise 2: Word Choice

Cross out the underlined word and replace it with another word from the TEACH domain that has a similar meaning.

Example: My parents ~~taught~~ ? me at home the first four years of my life.

Ex. _____educated_____

1. While the professor was explaining ? the organization of cellular life forms, several students started to doze off.

    1. _____

2. Some parents think there is real value in paying someone to coach ? their children for college entrance exams.

    2. _____

3. A good teacher can illustrate ? a science experiment with lively examples and a great deal of classroom participation.

    3. _____

4. It's not easy to lead a discussion ? . Not only do you have to be a good speaker, but you also have to be a good listener.

    4. _____

5. Michael didn't understand a word the professor said about quantum theory. He asked the teacher to review ? the concept one more time.

    5. _____

V. Introducing the Domain

The LEARN Domain

Teach and learn are two sides of the same coin. Teachers teach and students learn. Of course, it's not quite as simple as that. There are many different ways to learn. Some verbs in the LEARN domain are presented in the chart below. Look over the chart and mark any words that you don't know.

The LEARN Domain

learn
learn about
acquire knowledge (of)
gain knowledge (of)

master

memorize
learn by heart
commit to memory

absorb
pick up

review
go over
practice

VI. Exploring the Domain

A. When we learn, we acquire knowledge of something that we didn't know before or we add to the knowledge that we already have. We put new information in our brain. We can gain knowledge of something in a formal classroom situation or from life experience. In fact, some people think that life is the best teacher of all!

　　In your opinion, what is one subject that you need to gain knowledge of in a classroom? What is another subject that you can acquire knowledge of from life or experience?

> learn
> learn about
> acquire knowledge (of)
> gain knowledge (of)

B. Sometimes we can learn without having to make a tremendous effort. It's possible, for example, to pick up another language without formally studying it. If you live in a new country, you need to communicate with people. You will absorb the new information around you and before you even realize it, you will have learned many new words.

　　What do you think is the best way to pick up a language?

> pick up
> absorb

C. Often when we learn new information, particularly in school, we have to find a way to put it in our brains and keep it there! One time-honored way to do this is to memorize the information. We study it again and again, looking at the page until we have learned it by heart. Students all over the world spend a fair amount of time committing whole pages of facts and figures to memory. Some people memorize by copying the material, others by repeating it out loud over and over.

　　Which method do you use? What is the most difficult thing you have ever had to learn by heart?

> memorize
> learn by heart
> commit to memory

D. Some educators say that the best time to review or go over material is half an hour before you go to sleep or half an hour after you wake up.

　　It's also important to practice new skills. If you are learning to play the violin, you might want to practice an hour every day. Learning a new language requires practice, too.

　　When are you going to go over the vocabulary words you learned today?

> review
> go over
> practice

E. How long does it take to learn something completely? It probably wouldn't take you very long to master a skill like typing. However, it might take you many years to master the skills and knowledge needed to perform brain surgery!

　　What knowledge or skill do you think you have mastered? Have you ever taught it to anyone else?

> master

VII. Exercises

Exercise 3: Beginning Practice

In each group of words below, circle the two words or expressions that have the most similar meanings.

1. acquire knowledge of   master   gain knowledge of

2. absorb   memorize   pick up   master

3. learn by heart   memorize   gain knowledge of   pick up

Exercise 4: Word Choice

Complete the sentences with the best word from the list. Pay attention to verb forms.

master	memorize	absorb	go over
acquire knowledge of	learn by heart	pick up	practice
gain knowledge of	commit to memory	learn about	

1. Michelle wants to be a veterinarian. She knows that animals' lives will depend on her skill and knowledge. That's why she wants to _?_ every aspect of animal behavior and health.

    1. _____

2. We live in a very computerized society. For this reason, we use lots of numbers every day: our social security number, our automatic teller code, our driver's license number. These are numbers that we have to _?_ .

    2. _____

3. Gina studied Italian for two years in college, but she could barely speak a word of it. Then, she spent a year living and studying in Italy. She spent her first three months there _?_ the language by listening to people's conversations and watching TV.

    3. _____

4. If you want to _?_ a difficult topic, you will probably want to get some formal instruction. Some people can teach themselves from books, but most of us need more than that. We need someone to explain it to us, too.

    4. _____

5. Some people think it is possible to learn while you are sleeping. What do you think? Is it possible to _?_ difficult technical concepts by listening to a tape while you are sleeping?

    5. _____

6. In some elementary schools in the United States, students are expected to stand up and say the "Gettysburg Address" by Abraham Lincoln or the Preamble to the U.S. Constitution. Some of the children have to struggle for hours to _?_ famous speeches or writings.

    6. _____

7. Poor Talal! He really attended "the school of hard knocks"! This means that he has experienced many difficulties in life and learned some hard lessons by making mistakes. This is one very hard way to _?_ life.

    7. _____

Exercise 5: Sentence Completion

This exercise uses words from both the TEACH and LEARN domains. Choose the best word to complete the sentence and write it on the line.

1. When there are 100 students in a class, it is difficult to have a discussion. So, the professor usually __?__ . (*lectures, absorbs, educates*)

2. As the teacher led a discussion on human rights, the students were also __?__ how to listen to each other better. (*training, learning, memorizing*)

3. It was easy for Phil to get a high score on the SAT because his older brother had __?__ him in test-taking strategies. (*picked up, memorized, tutored*)

4. The biology teacher performed the dissection of the frog. The students watched her and after she had __?__ the correct way to do it, she let the students try it on their own. (*gained knowledge of, modeled, picked up*)

5. *Sam:* Oh, no! We have a big economics test tomorrow and I can't understand any of this stuff!

   Claire: Are you going to __?__ it tonight? I can help you. Maybe we can study together. (*coach, go over, educate*)

6. I really had two kinds of education. At school, I gained knowledge of reading, writing, and arithmetic, and at home my parents __?__ me about how to get along with people. (*learned by heart, educated, picked up*)

7. Teaching vocabulary isn't easy, and learning it isn't easy either! It's not so hard to master the words for concrete objects (table, airplane, baby), but abstract concepts (love, peace, kindness) can be difficult for a teacher to __?__ . Each language may have a slightly different way of referring to them. (*present, lead a discussion, train*)

8. You probably won't be surprised to learn that students often pay more attention to what other students say than to what the teacher says. It can be more effective for a student to __?__ to do something rather than the teacher. (*drill, gain knowledge of, show how*)

1. _____

2. _____

3. _____

4. _____

5. _____

6. _____

7. _____

8. _____

Exercise 6: Word Choice

Part A

What do you think is the best way to learn each of the things listed below? Choose a word from the LEARN domain and write it on the line.

1. to play a song on the piano _____

2. important dates in history _____

3. art appreciation _____

4. to type more quickly _____

5. new vocabulary words _____

Part B

What do you think is the best way to teach the following things? Choose a word from the TEACH domain and write it on the line.

1. Einstein's Theory of Relativity

2. multiplication tables

3. penalty kicks (in soccer)

4. cardiopulmonary resuscitation (CPR)

1. _____

2. _____

3. _____

4. _____

Exercise 7: For Discussion or Writing

Individually or in a group, answer these questions.

1. In your country, is it more common for a high school teacher to lecture or to lead a discussion? Which do you prefer?

2. Do students in your country spend a lot of time memorizing information? What kind of information do they have to learn by heart?

3. In your high school or college, did students form study groups in which they went over material together? Or was it more usual for students to review for tests on their own?

4. If a student in your country is having difficulty mastering a subject, what can be done? Does another student or teacher tutor that student? How much do people usually pay for one hour of tutoring?

5. What sports do high school students in your country participate in? Which sports have teams? Who coaches these teams? How often do they have training sessions after school?

VIII. Expanding the Domain

Noun Forms

Many of the verbs in the TEACH domain also have a noun form that refers to the person who does that kind of teaching. For many of these words in the TEACH domain the noun is formed by adding the suffixes -er or -or. However, there are some exceptions!

Exercise 8: Dictionary Work

Find the correct noun to complete each one of the following sentences. If necessary, use a dictionary or ask other students or the teacher.

Example: A person who <u>teaches</u> students is a <u> ? </u> .

1. A person who <u>educates</u> others is an <u> ? </u> .

Ex. _____ teacher

1. _____

2. A person who <u>instructs</u> students is an __?__ .

2. _____

3. A person who <u>gives lectures</u> is a __?__ .

3. _____

4. A person who <u>presents</u> information is a __?__ .

4. _____

5. A person who <u>leads</u> a discussion is a discussion __?__ .

5. _____

6. A person who <u>facilitates</u> a discussion is a __?__ .

6. _____

7. A person who <u>tutors</u> others is a __?__ .

7. _____

8. A person who <u>coaches</u> a soccer team is a soccer __?__ .

8. _____

9. A person who <u>trains</u> people in public speaking is a __?__ .

9. _____

Exercise 9: Dictionary Work

Some words in the TEACH and LEARN domains have related nouns that refer to the activity itself. Find the correct noun to complete each of the following sentences. Use a dictionary or ask others, if necessary.

You will notice that many of these nouns end in the suffix *-ion,* but once again, there are exceptions!

Example: To <u>educate</u> is to provide an __?__ .

Ex. _____education_____

1. To <u>instruct</u> is to provide __?__ .

1. _____

2. To <u>explain</u> is to give an __?__ .

2. _____

3. To <u>present</u> is to give a __?__ .

3. _____

4. To <u>demonstrate</u> is to give a __?__ .

4. _____

5. To <u>model</u> is to provide a __?__ .

5. _____

6. To <u>illustrate</u> is to give an __?__ .

6. _____

7. To <u>drill</u> is to provide a __?__ .

7. _____

8. To <u>memorize</u> something is to learn it through __?__ .

8. _____

Exercise 10: For Discussion or Writing

Individually or in a group, answer these questions.

1. If you could magically change one thing about the educational system in your country, what would you change?

2. How is the educational system in your country different from the educational system in the U.S.?

Love Makes the World Go Round

THE LOVE—HATE DOMAIN

I. Getting Ready

The title of this unit, "Love Makes the World Go 'Round," is a common expression in English. People say this because they think love is an important emotion. They think that love makes things happen. Unfortunately, hate is also a common emotion in today's world.

Discuss the following questions with your whole class or in a small group.

1. What are some of the ways we can see love and hate expressed in the world today?
2. What is the difference between liking and loving? Between disliking and hating?
3. Which emotion do you feel more often, like or love? Hate or love?

II. Introducing the Domain

There are many English verbs that describe feelings of love, like, dislike, and hate. How many do you already know? Fill in the chart on the next page with as many verbs as you can think of. Do this exercise in a small group and exchange ideas as you fill in the chart. Put any informal verbs in the correct column at the bottom of the chart.

Love   **Like**   **Dislike**   **Hate**

■ *Informal*   ■ *Informal*

Now compare your chart to the one below. How many words and expressions from this domain do you already know? Mark the ones that you don't know.

The LOVE—HATE Domain

Love	**Like**	**Dislike**	**Hate**
love	like	dislike	hate
cherish	enjoy	disapprove of	detest
treasure	care for	not care for	despise
prize	be fond of	object to	loathe
	find someone or	have no use for	abhor
adore	something pleasant	have no taste for	
idolize	feel tenderness for	take a dislike to	
revere	feel affection for		
worship	feel an attraction for		

■ *Informal*
be nuts about
be crazy about
dig

■ *Informal*
can't stand
hate someone's guts
have it in for

III. Exploring the Domain

LOVE—LIKE

Let's look first at the words and expressions for loving and liking.

A. Mrs. Jackson is my neighbor. I adore her because she is considerate, witty, and charming. She cherishes her three grandchildren. In her living room is a picture she treasures. It is a picture of all her children and grandchildren. She prizes it because her whole family is rarely together.

> love
> cherish
> treasure
> prize
>
> adore
> idolize
> revere
> worship

B. Many people get excited about movie stars and famous singers. My older sister adores Elvis Presley. She idolizes him and reads everything she can about him. She reveres every song that he sang. She almost worships the house that he lived in.

C. Nature-lovers are people who love nature. They feel affection for the plants and animals that live in the woods. They genuinely care for the wildlife found in natural areas. That's why they want stronger laws to protect the environment.

> like
> enjoy
> care for
> be fond of
> find someone or some-
>   thing pleasant
> feel tenderness for
> feel affection for
> feel an attraction for

My neighbors are nature-lovers. They find it pleasant to hike in the woods, observing the plants and animals around them. There is nothing they enjoy more than watching a deer eating grass in a meadow. They feel a great tenderness for the animals of the forest.

Although I don't consider myself a real nature-lover, I do feel an attraction for the cool beauty of a green forest on a hot summer day.

D. There's a really gorgeous girl who sits next to me in economics class. We talk to each other a lot before class. I'm nuts about her. I dig the way she dresses and I'm crazy about the way she smiles. I'm going to ask her out this weekend.

> be nuts about
> be crazy about
> dig

IV. Exercises

> ## LOVE—LIKE

Exercise 1: Beginning Practice

Cross out the word that doesn't belong.

1. care for   be fond of   revere

2. be nuts about   enjoy   be crazy about

3. feel tenderness for   revere   worship

4. dig   prize   adore

5. treasure   care for   cherish

Exercise 2: Word Choice

Choose the word or expression that best completes the sentence and write it on the line. Be ready to explain your choices. More than one answer might be correct for some sentences.

1. Carrie has an album of pictures that her mother gave her. In the album are pictures of her great-grandmother, her paternal grandmother and grandfather, and her mother as a child. Carrie __?__ this album. (*treasures, feels affection for, cares for*)

1. _____

2. Diego went to a movie last week. He really __?__ it because it was about baseball, his favorite sport. (*revered, idolized, enjoyed*)

2. _____

3. On cool summer evenings I __?__ outside with my friends. (*find it pleasant to sit, am crazy about sitting, cherish sitting*)

3. _____

4. My older sister __?__ the Beatles. She listens to their music constantly and wears a T-shirt with their picture on it. (*worships, is nuts about, cherishes*)

4. _____

5. Hiroshi is on the high school soccer team. His coach, Al Kovacs, is a superb soccer player who really enjoys working with teenagers. Hiroshi __?__ Mr. Kovacs and wants to be like him when he is older. (*idolizes, cares for, enjoys*)

5. _____

6. Jason has called Megan every night this week. He took her to a movie last weekend and is taking her to a concert tonight. He says she's the greatest. He really __?__ her. (*is fond of, is crazy about, reveres*)

6. _____

7. I ? rock and roll music. It makes me feel good when I listen to it. (*prize, feel tenderness for, dig*)

7. _____

8. Irina has known Alex for a few weeks. She thinks he is intelligent and fun to be with. She ? Alex and would like to get to know him better. (*adores, is nuts about, is fond of*)

8. _____

V. Exploring the Domain

DISLIKE—HATE

Let's look at words and expressions for disliking and hating.

A. I like to think of myself as an open-minded person. But there are some things I hate. For one thing, I detest rude people. I despise people who cut into line in front of me or knock me over as they hurry by. I loathe corrupt governments that spend money on unnecessary things. And, although I am quite fond of most animals, I abhor snakes!

hate
detest
despise
loathe
abhor

B. Sometimes my feelings aren't quite as strong. For example, I don't hate violent movies, but I do object to them. I think they make society more violent. I also disapprove of people who don't obey traffic laws and I don't care for people who think they are better than everyone else. I have no taste for skiing. I took a dislike to it when I fell and broke my leg the first time I tried it. And I have no use for silly items like battery-powered nail files.

dislike	have no
disapprove	use for
of	have no
not care for	taste for
object to	take a
	dislike to

C. The conversation below took place on the playground of an elementary school. Teresa and Nick are both in the sixth grade.

Teresa: Nick, I hear you have it in for Jason because he stole your lunch yesterday. Do you really hate his guts? Are you going to get him after school today?"

Nick: Yeah, I can't stand guys like him who think they can get away with taking things from other people.

can't stand
hate someone's guts
have it in for

VI. Exercises

DISLIKE—HATE

Exercise 3: Beginning Practice

Study the words and expressions for DISLIKE and HATE for a few minutes. Then look at the list of words below. Write *D* (*dislike*) or *H* (*hate*). When you have finished, check your work by looking back at the domain.

_____ **1.** abhor

_____ **3.** detest

_____ **2.** object to

_____ **4.** take a dislike to

_____ **5.** not care for   _____ **8.** loathe

_____ **6.** have no use for   _____ **9.** have no taste for

_____ **7.** despise   _____ **10.** disapprove of

Exercise 4: Word Choice

Choose the word or expression that best completes the sentence and write it on the line. Be ready to explain your choices. More than one answer might be correct for some sentences.

1. My father is fond of dogs, but he _?_ cats. He thinks they don't make very good pets. (*abhors, has no use for, detests*)

2. A new family moved in next door to us last week. Unfortunately, my younger sister _?_ the children from the beginning. She says they were rude to her when she went over to play with them. (*had it in for, took a dislike to, abhorred*)

3. I have _?_ spiders every since the day my older brother scared me by putting one on my arm. (*loathed, objected to, had no taste for*)

4. My mother _?_ mini-skirts and bikinis. She prefers more conservative clothing. (*despises, detests, disapproves of*)

5. I _?_ drivers who follow too closely behind my car. Their tailgating makes me nervous. (*can't stand, have it in for, abhor*)

6. Victor got an A on the math test, but I know he cheated. I _?_ people who cheat. I think they should all get F's! (*despise, have no taste for, disapprove of*)

1. _____

2. _____

3. _____

4. _____

5. _____

6. _____

VII. Combined Exercises

The LOVE—HATE Domains

The following exercises use all the words you have learned in this unit.

Exercise 5: Reviewing the Domains

Put the words in each list into the correct column.

	LOVE	LIKE	DISLIKE	HATE
1. have no taste for	_____	_____	_____	_____
care for				
prize				
loathe				

	LOVE	LIKE	DISLIKE	HATE
2. abhor	_____	_____	_____	_____
feel tenderness for				
object to				
revere				
3. not care for	_____	_____	_____	_____
detest				
be fond of				
adore				
4. cherish	_____	_____	_____	_____
despise				
find something pleasant				
take a dislike to				

Exercise 6: Rhyming Words

Complete the following rhymes by adding a word from the LOVE–HATE domain that rhymes with (sounds the same as) the underlined word.

1. I can't tell you how I __?__
People who are always <u>late</u>.

2. I want to see you more and <u>more</u>,
For it is you I truly __?__ .

3. Spiders, snakes, robbers, and <u>lies</u>,
These are things I do __?__ .

4. I'm sending you a little <u>present</u>,
Because I __?__ you very __?__ .

5. By any <u>measure</u>,
It's you I __?__ .

6. From the rooftops I will <u>shout</u>,
You're the one I'm __?__ .

7. Some people like the sun and <u>sand</u>,
But the beach is something I __?__ .

1. _____

2. _____

3. _____

4. _____

_____

5. _____

6. _____

7. _____

Exercise 7: For Discussion

There are many different kinds of animals in the world. Some of them, like puppies and kittens, are cute and lovable. Others, like snakes, are disliked or even hated by many people. Look at the list of animals below. First, decide how you feel about each animal. Then choose a word from the LOVE–HATE domain that best describes your feelings. Discuss your answers with your classmates.

1. spiders _____

_____

2. baby rabbits _____

_____

3. puppies _____

_____

4. panda bears _____

_____

5. mice _____

_____

6. cats _____

_____

7. bees _____

_____

8. mosquitoes _____

_____

Exercise 8: Express Yourself

Part A

Marvin, the chubby baby in the cartoon, loves playing in mud, but hates taking baths. Think of eight activities that you either love, like, dislike, or hate doing. Put the names of those activities in the correct columns below. Use a gerund (verb+ -*ing*) to name the activities. For example, if you like <u>watching old movies on TV</u>, you would write that phrase in the column under LIKE.

Love	Like	Dislike	Hate

Part B

Now write eight sentences about these activities. In your sentences, try to use words from the LOVE–HATE domain that are new to you. Also, explain why you feel the way you do about these activities.

Example: I adore swimming on hot days because it cools me off.

Part C

In a small group, share some of your sentences. Try to find one or more activities that your group feels the same about. One member of your group should be ready to report to the whole class. Can you find an activity that the whole class feels the same about?

VIII. Expanding the Domain

Word Forms

Many of the verbs in the LOVE–HATE domain have adjective and noun forms, as given in the chart below.

Verb	Adjective (describes object or person that causes the feeling)	Noun (names the feeling)
love	lovable	love
adore	adorable	adoration
revere	_____	reverence
like	likable	liking
enjoy	enjoyable	enjoyment
hate	hateful	hatred/hate
detest	detestable	detestation
despise	despicable	
abhor	abhorrent	abhorrence
loathe	loathsome	loathing

Exercise 9: Sentence Completion

Choose the word or expression that best completes the sentence and then write the word on the line.

1. She received an __?__ stuffed animal for Valentine's Day. (*adore, adorable, adoration*)

   1. _____

2. Most people __?__ the events that took place in the concentration camps of Nazi Germany. (*abhorrence, abhor, abhorrent*)

   2. _____

3. People usually feel a sense of __?__ when they enter a church, mosque, temple, or shrine. (*revere, reverence*)

   3. _____

4. Acts of violence are often committed by people who are filled with __?__ . (*hateful, hatred*)

   4. _____

5. Fluffy white kittens are very __?__ . (*lovable, love*)

   5. _____

6. I don't like Fred at all. I think his attitude toward women is __?__ . (*despise, despicable*)

   6. _____

7. I __?__ people who are not honest. (*detest, detestable, detestation*)

   7. _____

8. The good company and good food heightened our __?__ of the evening. (*enjoy, enjoyable, enjoyment*)

   8. _____

Three American teenagers.

Exercise 10: For Discussion

In this chapter we have presented only some of the words in the LOVE–HATE domain. There are many informal words and expressions that we have not included. People, especially teenagers, are constantly creating new ways to say that they love or hate something or someone. If you listen to informal, conversational English, you will hear some of these words.

Ask your teacher or a native speaker of English about some current informal expressions that belong in this domain. Discuss them with your classmates.

Exercise 11: For Discussion

People often show that they like or dislike something through non-verbal communication (gestures, facial expressions, body movements, etc.). A smile seems to be a universal way to show that we like something. What are some non-verbal ways that people in your native country show that they like or dislike something or someone?

Exercise 12: For Writing or Discussion

Sigmund Freud, the founder of psychoanalysis, coined (created) the word "ambivalent." This word describes how we feel when we have conflicting feelings, such as love and hate, about something or someone. If you have ambivalent feelings about a person, you like and dislike that person, all at the same time. Have you ever felt ambivalent about a person or an event? Either orally or in writing, describe that person or event. Tell why you felt ambivalent.

152 ■ WALK, AMBLE, STROLL

Something Old, Something New

THE OLD—NEW DOMAIN

I. Getting Ready

Discuss the following questions with your whole class or in a small group.

1. Do you remember how you felt when you were a child and your parents bought you a new pair of shoes? Did you feel proud when you wore them to school for the first time? How long did they stay new? Now that you are older, do you prefer new shoes or old, comfortable ones?

2. Do you generally prefer old or new things? For example, would you rather live in a new apartment or in an older house? If you could buy a car, would you rather buy an old Mercedes or a new Ford?

II. Introducing the Domain

General Words

Because there are so many words in English that mean old or new, this unit has been divided into four domains. The first domain contains some general words for old and new. Look over the chart below and mark the words that you don't know.

General Words						
Old				**New**		
old	antique	ancient		new	recent	current	modern

The paragraph below will help you understand how these words are used.

Many people are interested in old things and events which happened a long time ago. Some of them like to buy expensive antique furniture and others enjoy reading books about Julius Caesar and other leaders from ancient history. Other people are more interested in new things and new ideas. They like to have modern furniture or read about current events. Some of them only go to the most recent movies.

Do you prefer old or new movies? Are you more interested in ancient or modern history?

III. Introducing the Domain

Condition

The next domain gives words which not only indicate the age of something, but also give us information about what condition it is in. For example, a broken-down car is not only old, it is also in bad condition.

Look at the chart on the next page and mark the words that you don't know.

Condition					
Old			**New**		
old	rusty	*Food*	new	*Food*	
broken-down	faded	stale	brand-new	fresh	
run-down	tattered	spoiled			
worn-down	threadbare	bad			
worn-out	moth-eaten				
decrepit		moldy			
dilapidated		rotten			
shabby		rancid			

IV. Exploring the Domain

Condition

A. *Old, Broken-Down, and Worn-Out.* Yuko and Takeru were on vacation in West Virginia. They had rented a cottage in the mountains. On Friday, they decided to go hiking in the woods near their cottage. As they were roaming through the woods, they stumbled on a broken-down old shack. It was so dilapidated that it looked like it might fall over at any moment. They wondered if anyone owned this decrepit place. Feeling adventurous, they decided to go inside.

> old
> broken-down
> run-down
> worn-down
> worn-out
> decrepit
> dilapidated
> shabby
>
> rusty
> faded
> tattered
> threadbare
> moth-eaten

The hinges on the door were rusty and the door creaked as they went in. The room they entered was dark, dirty, and shabby. In one corner was a moth-eaten sofa that was full of holes. Next to the sofa was an old lamp with a crooked, tattered shade. Everything was covered with dust and the curtains on the windows were faded and threadbare. In the kitchen, they could see a rusty refrigerator. It was obvious that no one had lived there for many years. Yuko felt uneasy wandering through the run-down house; it was gloomy and depressing. "Let's get out of here!" she whispered to Takeru. So they hurried out of the cabin into the fresh air and sunlight. They continued their walk, wondering about the story behind the old, abandoned cabin.

Have you ever seen a run-down cabin like the one described in this paragraph? If you came across one, would you go into it?

B. *Really New.* Sometimes English speakers want to emphasize the newness of something. They do this by saying that it is brand new. If a child gets a new sweater for his birthday, one that has never been worn by anyone else, he might say it is a brand-new sweater. But young children often wear their older brothers' or sisters' clothes when the older brothers and sisters have grown too big for them. We call these clothes hand-me-downs.

new brand-new

C. *Fresh Food—Old Food.* Fresh food is delicious, but stale food tastes bad. It can even make you sick. Refrigerators help keep food fresh, but even in a refrigerator food can go bad if it is not used soon enough.

Have you ever found rotten, spoiled food in your refrigerator?

Some of the words that describe old food are used only with certain kinds of food. For example, when butter is too old to eat, we say it is rancid, but when meat goes bad, we say it is rotten. The list below matches these words with the kinds of old food they usually describe.

stale	fresh
spoiled	
bad	
moldy	
rotten	
rancid	

Old Food	
stale	bread, cake, baked goods
moldy	bread, cake, cheese, fruit
rotten	meat, fruit, vegetables
rancid	butter, margarine, oil, nuts

It is important to know how long different kinds of food stay fresh. Bread can become stale in only a few days. Cheese gets moldy in a week or two. Ground meat becomes rotten quickly. If it is not used in two or three days, it should be put in the freezer. Oil stays fresh for a long time if it is stored properly, but becomes rancid if it is kept in a warm place.

V. Exercises

Condition

Exercise 1: Dictionary Work

Part A

Some of the words in this domain give us information about why an old thing is in bad condition. Knowing the meanings of the words below will help you understand some of the words in this domain. Look up in your dictionary the words that you don't know and write down their definitions.

1. mold _____

2. to rust _____

3. to fade _____

4. to tatter _____

5. a thread _____

6. bare (adjective) _____

7. a moth _____

Part B

Now complete the sentences below with a word from the list.

moldy	rusty	faded
tattered	threadbare	moth-eaten

1. An old sofa covered with fabric that is so worn that its threads are showing is __?__ .

2. An old coat that has tiny holes in it is __?__ .

3. A piece of old cheese that has mold on it is __?__ .

4. An old suit whose colors are no longer bright is __?__ .

5. An old car that has been left outside for many years becomes __?__ .

6. An old blouse that is worn and ragged is __?__ .

1. _____

2. _____

3. _____

4. _____

5. _____

6. _____

Exercise 2: Word Choice

Circle the letter of the word that best describes the objects described below.

1. A bowl of chicken soup that has been in the refrigerator for a month. . .
(a) recent (b) run-down (c) rotten

2. A dinosaur bone that is two million years old. . .
(a) ancient (b) decrepit (c) rancid

3. A cheap plastic wallet that has been used for four years. . .
(a) brand new (b) current (c) shabby

4. A boat that was built 30 years ago and has never been painted or repaired. . .
(a) moth-eaten (b) ancient (c) dilapidated

5. Lettuce that was picked three hours ago. . .
   (a) antique (b) spoiled (c) fresh

6. A dress that has been washed over and over again for many years. . .
   (a) modern (b) threadbare (c) broken-down

Exercise 3: Word Choice

Cross out the word <u>old</u> or <u>new</u> in the sentences below and write another word from the domains.

Example: Poor people often live in ̶o̶l̶d̶ ? tenements.   Ex. _____run-down_____

1. I bought a beautiful, old ? table that was made in the 18th century in France.   1. _____

2. My car is old ? , but I can't afford to buy a new one.   2. _____

3. When his television stopped working he bought a new ? one.   3. _____

4. We had to throw the butter away because it was old ? .   4. _____

5. These jeans are old ? . There are holes at the knees.   5. _____

6. The man's house was old ? , but he was too sick to repair it and paint it.   6. _____

7. Vegetables lose their vitamins as they get older. They are highest in nutrition when they are new ? .   7. _____

8. This swimsuit is so old ? that I can't wear it anymore.   8. _____

9. The magazines in the waiting room of my dentist's office are usually several months old, but I only like to read the new ? issue of a magazine.   9. _____

10. When bread gets old ? , we often feed it to the birds.   10. _____

VI. Introducing the Domain

Style

Do teenagers in your country worry about the kind of clothes they wear? Do they want their clothes to be modern and fashionable? Do they spend a lot of money on stylish clothes?

The words in this domain are used to talk about clothes, hairstyles, furniture, ideas, or anything else that involves style. These are things that are usually in style when they are new and become old-fashioned as they get older. Look over the chart below and mark the words that you don't know.

Style			
Old		**New**	
old	outdated	new	chic
old-fashioned	dated	fashionable	stylish
outmoded	dowdy	in style	modern
		in vogue	contemporary
		up-to-date	

VII. Exploring the Domain

Style

It's hard to keep up with fashion. What is fashionable one day is outmoded the next. A suit that was stylish and contemporary when your grandmother wore it 30 years ago would seem quite dowdy today. The mini-skirt was very chic for a few years and then became out-dated. But in the late 1980s, it was suddenly in vogue again. What was old-fashioned one day became modern and contemporary the next.

Hairstyles come and go as well. In the 1960s, it was stylish for women in the United States to wear their hair in a long, straight style. In the 1970s, that hairstyle became dated and short, curly hair was considered more up-to-date.

Do fashions change quickly in your country? What about hairstyles? Do they change as quickly as fashions?

old-fashioned	fashionable
outmoded	in style
outdated	in vogue
dated	up-to-date
dowdy	chic
	stylish
	modern
	contemporary

VIII. Exercises

Style

Exercise 4: Beginning Practice

Cross out the word that doesn't belong.

1. outdated   chic   dowdy

2. stylish   outmoded   fashionable

3. contemporary   in vogue   dated

4. old-fashioned   up-to-date   in style

Exercise 5: Sentence Completion

Complete these sentences with words from the domain. There are some clues to help you.

1. He's a bright, c __ __ __ __ __ __ __ __ __ __ __ man.

   His clothes are always u __ - t __ - d __ __ __ .

2. She's an o __ __ - f __ __ __ __ __ __ __ __ woman. She

   wears clothes that are o __ __ d __ __ __ __ and her ideas are

   o __ __ m __ __ __ __ , too.

3. I like m __ __ __ __ __ houses because of their clean lines and

   uncluttered look.

4. Monica, a college student, wouldn't think of borrowing her mother's

   clothes. She thinks they are old and d __ __ __ __ .

Exercise 6: For Discussion

Sometimes a style or kind of clothing becomes very popular for a short period of time. We call this a "fad." Hairstyles, words, and behaviors can become fads. For example, many students in a high school might suddenly begin to wear white shirts with multicolored buttons. Those shirts could be called a fad. But a few months later, the white shirts could be out and bright orange and green shoelaces could be in. Fads go in and out of style quickly.

1. Give an example of something that has become a fad in the United States or in your country.

2. How do you think fads get started?

3. Do you think that the manufacturers of some products try to start fads? If so, how do they do this? Why?

IX. Introducing the Domain

> ### Obsolete—Innovative

Sometimes a thing is not just old-fashioned, it's also <u>obsolete</u>. Obsolete means that an object is no longer useful because something better has been created. A good example is the slide rule. This instrument was used in the past for mathematical calculations, but the modern calculator has made it <u>obsolete</u>.

Look over the chart below and mark the words that you don't know.

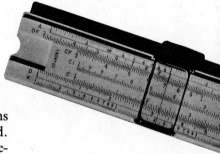

A slide rule.

Old	New
old	new
obsolete	innovative
obsolescent	modern
outmoded	up-to-date
	high-technology
	high-tech
	state-of-the-art
	on the cutting edge

X. Exploring the Domain

Obsolete—Innovative

There is a lot of competition among high-technology companies today. Engineers must create innovative, up-to-date products in order to keep their companies on the cutting edge. In high-technology fields such as computers and telecommunications, state-of-the-art equipment, equipment that is the best and most advanced, can quickly become outmoded or obsolete. In order to compete in these high-tech fields, companies must continually come up with innovative products and ideas.

XI. Exercises

An array of radiotelescopes.

Obsolete—Innovative

Exercise 7: Beginning Practice

Add a word in each group that is similar in meaning.

1. outmoded, old, _____

2. up-to-date, on the cutting edge, _____

3. modern, high-tech, _____

Exercise 8: For Discussion

Working with a partner, choose an adjective from the domain to describe each of these objects.

1. a feather pen

   _____

2. the space shuttle

   _____

3. hand-held computers

   _____

4. telephones that show a picture of the person you are talking to

   _____

5. an icebox (a large box made of wood which uses a big block of ice to keep food cold)

   _____

Exercise 9: For Discussion

In a small group, talk about some other objects that are obsolete or innovative. Try to use as many words from the domain as you can in your discussion.

XII. Exercises

The following exercises will give you practice with all the words from this unit.

Exercise 10: Reviewing the Domain

Put each word from the list into its correct place in the chart of the OLD–NEW domain.

high-technology	chic	stale
dowdy	recent	decrepit
worn-down	brand new	tattered
stylish	dated	ancient
fresh	obsolescent	state-of-the-art
in vogue	current	antique

	Old	New
General	_____	_____
	_____	_____
Condition	_____	_____
	_____	_____
	_____	_____
	_____	_____
Style	_____	_____
	_____	_____
		_____
Obsolete/ Innovative	_____	_____
		_____

Exercise 11: Word Choice

Choose the word from the domain that best completes the sentence and write it on the line. Be ready to explain your choice.

1. I don't think you should buy that car. It looks pretty ＿?＿ to me. (*obsolete, rusty, dowdy*)

   1. _____

2. We'd better throw these grapes away. They don't look very ＿?＿ . (*modern, up-to-date, fresh*)

   2. _____

3. I'm going to ask for a more ＿?＿ hairstyle the next time I get my hair cut. (*fashionable, high-tech, state-of-the-art*)

   3. _____

4. That computer company hires engineers who have ＿?＿ ideas. (*stylish, brand new, innovative*)

   4. _____

5. Maria wrote an angry letter to the owner of the store where she bought her new sweater. The sweater was ＿?＿ after being washed only five times. (*obsolescent, outmoded, worn out*)

   5. _____

6. Tim decided it was time to buy a new suit. The edges of the sleeves of his old suit were getting _?_ . (*tattered, outdated, rancid*)

6. _____

7. Andrea's new house is beautiful. Her interior decorator helped her buy _?_ furniture. (*fresh, stylish, on the cutting edge*)

7. _____

8. We'd better not eat that yogurt. It looks _?_ . (*run-down, moldy, decrepit*)

8. _____

9. It can be dangerous to go into _?_ houses because they are no longer in safe condition. (*rancid, dated, dilapidated*)

9. _____

10. The city council decided to repair the bathrooms in the housing project. Many of them were _?_ . (*broken-down, faded, threadbare*)

10. _____

Exercise 12: For Discussion or Writing

Some people are completely old-fashioned. They wear outdated clothes and have old-fashioned, conservative ideas. They like to live in old houses and drive ancient cars. There are other people who are always up-to-date. At work they use state-of-the-art computers and have innovative ideas. At home they like to watch the latest movies and they wear fashionable clothes. But not everyone is completely old-fashioned or completely up-to-date. Some people are modern in some ways and old-fashioned in others. They like to combine the old and the new. Do you know anyone like this? Can you describe this person? Why do you think this person combines the old and the new?

UNIT 17

It's a Wonderful LIFE

THE STAGES OF LIFE DOMAIN

I. Getting Ready

> What walks on four legs in the morning, two legs at noon, and three legs in the evening?

This puzzling question is called the "Riddle of the Sphinx." The answer to the riddle will give you an idea of what this unit is about. (If you can't solve this riddle with your classmates, look on page 178.)

In the United States, the most common family unit is the nuclear family, which includes parents and their children. But in many countries, the extended family is more common. The extended family includes children, parents, grandparents, and even great-grandparents, aunts, and uncles. In an extended family, many generations live together. The members of an extended family probably represent many of the stages of life. In English, these stages are called childhood, adolescence, adulthood, and old age.

Discuss the following question with your whole class or in a small group: How old are people when they are in childhood, adolescence, adulthood, and old age?

II. Creating the Domain

There are many words and expressions in English that identify one of the stages of life. Read each sentence below carefully. Then put the underlined word or words in the correct place on the chart.

Beginnings	Childhood	Adolescence	Adulthood	Old Age	Death

1. The birth of a baby is an exciting event for the whole family.
2. Childhood usually means the years when a child is in elementary school, from age five to twelve. When we say early childhood, we usually mean a child from one to five years of age.
3. Adolescence comes between childhood and adulthood. It can be a difficult time for some young people.
4. In most parts of the United States, adulthood legally begins at age eighteen.
5. Because of better health care, the stage of life called old age is coming later in people's lives.
6. Because many people don't like to say the word "death," they use other expressions like passing on or passing away. These words are called euphemisms.
7. In some cultures, boys and girls go through a ceremony when they reach manhood or womanhood.
8. During the teenage years, children often become more and more independent.
9. The first chapter of the Bible is called "Genesis" because it tells about the origin of life.
10. We begin to learn to read and write in our youth.
11. In the United States, the demise of a family member brings the extended family together for a funeral.
12. During their declining years, some people find they can no longer take care of themselves.
13. The creation of a new life is a miracle.
14. In our boyhood or girlhood, we often played with toys.
15. My grandmother is in the twilight of life, but she is still a happy, active person.
16. Puberty is the time when we become sexually mature.
17. During infancy we learn to walk and talk.
18. Those who oppose abortion say that life begins at the time of conception.
19. Some people think the prime of life is when we are 35 to 40 years old. Others think the prime of life comes later, from 45 to 50.
20. The decease of a close friend can cause feelings of depression and emptiness.

Below is how a native speaker of English might fill out the chart.

The STAGES OF LIFE Domain

Beginnings	**Childhood**	**Adolescence**	**Adulthood**	**Old Age**	**Death**
birth	childhood	adolescence	adulthood	old age	death
origin	youth	teenage years	womanhood	declining years	passing on
creation	boyhood	puberty	manhood	twilight of life	passing away
conception	girlhood		prime of life		demise
					decease

Early
infancy

III. Exercises

The STAGES OF LIFE Domain

Exercise 1: Beginning Practice

Put the words and expressions in each line in the correct order starting with BIRTH and going to DEATH.

BIRTH ⟵————————————————————⟶ DEATH

1. adolescence   adulthood   childhood

_____   _____   _____

2. puberty   decease   origin

_____   _____   _____

3. prime of life   girlhood   declining years   creation

_____   _____   _____   _____

4. infancy   demise   conception   teenage years   manhood

_____   _____   _____   _____   _____

5. twilight of life   passing away   boyhood   birth   womanhood

_____   _____   _____   _____   _____

Exercise 2: Analogies

Look at the example of an analogy given below.

Example: Hot is to cold as up is to __?__ .

Ex. _____down_____

In an analogy, two words are related in some way. In this example, hot is the opposite of cold. This analogy is completed by finding a word that is related to up in the same way hot is related to cold. Since down is the opposite of up, it completes the analogy. Be careful. The first two words will not always be opposites. In the example below, the words are synonyms.

Example: Birth is to creation as manhood is to ___?___ .

Ex. _____adulthood_____

Complete the analogies below with a word from the STAGES OF LIFE domain.

1. Decease is to prime of life as passing away is to ___?___ .

1. _____

2. Girlhood is to youth as demise is to ___?___ .

2. _____

3. Origin is to adolescence as conception is to ___?___ .

3. _____

4. Boyhood is to womanhood as childhood is to ___?___ .

4. _____

5. Teenage years is to declining years as puberty is to ___?___ .

5. _____

Exercise 3: Reading a Chart

The chart below gives information about some famous monarchs. These kings or queens usually came to the throne (became monarchs) upon the death of their father or mother. Some of them became king in their youth and others in their declining years. Many reigned (ruled) until their demise.

After looking at the chart, answer the questions below.

FAMOUS MONARCHS

NAME	Lifespan	Length of reign	Years of reign	Age at death
Tutankhamen of Egypt	1370–1352 B.C.	9 years	1361–1352 B.C.	18
John I of France	several days	several days	1316	several days
Edward V of England	1470–1483	about 70 days	1483	12
Elizabeth I of England	1533–1603	45 years	1558–1603	70
Louis XIV of France	1638–1715	72 years	1643–1715	76
Stanislaus of Poland	1677–1766	5 years	1704–1709	88
Peter II of Russia	1715–1730	3 years	1727–1730	14

1. Which king began to reign in his boyhood?

1. _____

2. Which monarch died in his infancy?

2. _____

3. Which king ruled during his manhood?

3. _____

4. Which monarchs ruled until their demise?

4. _____

5. Which person was a monarch in his/her teenage years?

5. _____

6. Who was a king from his youth to his decease?

6. _____

7. Which kings died during their teenage years?

7. _____

8. Which monarchs did not rule during their adolescence?

8. _____

Exercise 4: A Special Challenge

The Stages of Life in Literature

The following passage is from a well-known play by William Shakespeare called "As You Like It." In this passage Shakespeare describes the stages of life. With your teacher, read the passage. Don't worry if there are some parts of it that you don't understand. Just try to get a general idea of how Shakespeare describes each stage of life.

All the world's a stage,
And all the men and women merely[1] players:
They have their exits and their entrances;
And one man in his time plays many parts,

. . .At first the infant,   5
Mewling[2] and puking[3] in the nurse's arms.

And then the whining schoolboy, with his satchel,[4]
And shining morning face, creeping like snail
Unwillingly to school.

     And then the lover,
Sighing like furnace, with a woeful[5] ballad[6]   10
Made to his mistress' eyebrow.

. . .And then the justice,
In fair round belly with good capon[7] lin'd,
With eyes severe and beard of formal cut,. . .

And so he plays his parts. The sixth[8] age shifts   15
Into the lean and slipper'd pantaloon,
With spectacles on nose and pouch on side,
His youthful hose well sav'd a world too wide
For his shrunk shank[9]; and his big manly voice,
Turning again towards childish treble[10], pipes   20
And whistles in his sound.

     Last scene of all,
That ends this strange eventful history,
Is second childishness, and mere oblivion,
Sans[11] teeth, sans eyes, sans taste, sans everything.

[1]only   [2]crying   [3]vomiting   [4]bag   [5]sad   [6]song   [7]chicken   [8]One age has been omitted.   [9]part of leg   [10]high-pitched voice   [11]without

Part A

Write six words from the domain that describe the stages of life as Shakespeare saw them.

1. _____

2. _____

3. _____

4. _____

5. _____

6. _____

Part B

Looking again at Shakespeare's descriptions of each stage, which one do you think is the most flattering? Which one is the least flattering? Discuss your choices in a small group.

Most flattering: _____

Least flattering: _____

Part C

What stage of life is the most important in your own culture? What do people do to show that this particular stage of life is valued?

IV. Introducing the Domain

People of a Certain Age

English has many nouns that identify people according to their age. For example, we can say:

> The baby cried all night.
> That child is going to spill her milk.
> Adults are supposed to be more responsible than teenagers.

You probably already know many nouns like baby, child, adult, and teenager. With your classmates and teacher, think of as many words as you can that identify people according to their age.

Some of the more common words in this domain are given in the chart on the next page. How many of them do you already know? Look over the words in the chart and mark any that you don't know.

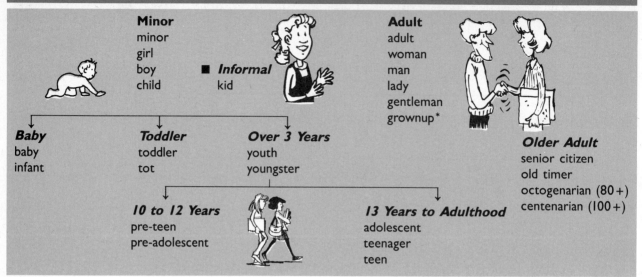

People of a Certain Age

Minor
minor
girl
boy
child

■ *Informal*
kid

Adult
adult
woman
man
lady
gentleman
grownup*

Baby
baby
infant

Toddler
toddler
tot

Over 3 Years
youth
youngster

Older Adult
senior citizen
old timer
octogenarian (80+)
centenarian (100+)

10 to 12 Years
pre-teen
pre-adolescent

13 Years to Adulthood
adolescent
teenager
teen

*Grownup is usually spelled grown-up when used as an adjective.

V. Exploring the Domain

People of a Certain Age

One way that some American families stay in touch with each other is by having a family reunion. All the members of the extended family agree to meet in one place for a few days. They come from all over the United States.

At a family reunion, you will see lots of children and adults. There will probably be several whimpering babies, as well as several delighted octogenarians!

The Reed family gets together every year. This year's reunion is really special because Gen Reed and her husband, Bill, are celebrating their 50th wedding anniversary on the day of the reunion, June 15. Everybody is outside, in the ⁵ backyard of the Reed's townhouse. Bill calls out, "Ladies and gentlemen! Come and get your cake!"

One of the little boys is chasing one of the little girls and trying to pull her hair. The little girl runs to tell her mother, but her mother is holding a sleeping baby. The infant is only two months old. "Shh, Kate!" the mother ¹⁰ whispers. "Don't wake the baby."

Kate runs off and joins the other youngsters who are running around. They accidentally knock down a ten-month-old who is learning to walk. The toddler immediately starts screaming. Another tot joins in. One of the adults yells, "Hey, kids! Stop running around. You'll hurt somebody!" One of the kids turns ¹⁵ to him and says, "Hey, Uncle Steve, you can't tell me what to do just because you're a grownup!"

Some older children are sitting on the grass eating some of the anniversary cake. They look bored. Two pre-teens are talking about how they can't wait

to get back home. Pre-adolescents rarely get excited about spending time with relatives. A few of the teenagers are inside watching a movie on TV.

Outside, Mrs. Reed's daughter is saying, "Having two adolescents in the house is horrendous! For one thing, I can never use the telephone. They're always on the phone talking to other teens who live right in our neighborhood!"

"That's nothing," says her younger brother. "You don't know how bad it can be. Can you believe this? My son just got arrested for shoplifting. Fortunately, he's not eighteen yet, so they charged him as a minor. I hope it doesn't hurt his chances of getting into Harvard."

Mrs. Reed's older sister is 83. She is sitting in a comfortable lounge chair and grinning peacefully at the noisy crowd of people. She remembers the big family reunions she went to long, long ago, when she was a youth. Now she's an octogenarian, but she looks much younger. She is interested in everything around her. She doesn't like people to think of her as a senior citizen. She would like to live to be 100. What a party the family could have then—for the first centenarian in the family.

VI. Exercises

Exercise 5: Beginning Practice

Put the words and expressions in each line in the correct order starting with BABY and going to OLDER ADULT.

BABY ◄————————————► OLDER ADULT

1. youth, tot, old-timer, gentleman ___ ___ ___ ___

2. adolescent, centenarian, infant, grownup ___ ___ ___ ___

3. senior citizen, toddler, youngster, lady ___ ___ ___ ___

Exercise 6: Word Choice

Complete the sentence with a word from the domain chart on page 172.

1. Ronald Reagan was elected when he was 69 years old. He became President of the United States when he was a/an   ?   .

2. Some Americans were so eager to fight in the Civil War that they joined the army when they were only 14 or 15 years old. They were only   ? , but they were fighting in a dreadful war.

3. In the United States, it is illegal for a/an   ?   to drink alcohol.

4. A/an   ?   requires almost constant care from its mother or father for the first few months of its life.

5. A   ?   who does not attend school regularly is called "a truant."

6. In your country, is it common for   ?   who are still in high school to have part-time jobs?

7. Because many   ?   are retired and have small incomes, they are often given discounts at restaurants, stores, and theaters.

8. Some men open doors for women because they think ladies should go before   ? .

9. Some children under the age of three go to special pre-schools. Some of these   ?   stay there from 9 A.M. to 6 P.M. every day.

10. Many children like to pretend. They say things like, "When I'm a/an   ? , I'm going to be a pilot."

1. _____

2. _____

3. _____

4. _____

5. _____

6. _____

7. _____

8. _____

9. _____

10. _____

VII. Introducing the Domain

The YOUNG—OLD Domain

We say that a baby is young, an adult is grown-up, and a centenarian is elderly. The words young, grown-up, and elderly are adjectives that tell us about a person's age. These words and other adjectives and expressions for age are given in the chart below. Look over the chart and mark any words that you don't know.

The YOUNG—OLD Domain

About Young People	About Adults	About Older Adults
young	adult	old
youthful	grown-up	elderly
juvenile	middle-aged	on in years
immature	in one's prime	advanced in years
childlike	mature	senile
childish		
boyish	■ *Informal and negative*	■ *Positive*
girlish	over the hill	young at heart
	past one's prime	

VIII. Exploring the Domain

The YOUNG—OLD Domain

A. Mrs. Jones is a librarian. She enjoys working with <u>young</u> people and is in charge of the <u>juvenile</u> book section at the library. Once a week she has a story hour. She reads stories aloud to the children and leads discussions with them. The children are <u>immature</u> and sometimes ask <u>childish</u> questions, but Mrs. Jones doesn't mind. She likes their <u>youthful</u> enthusiasm.

Mrs. Wong, on the other hand, thinks libraries should be quiet. She dislikes the <u>girlish</u> giggles and <u>boyish</u> laughter that can be heard during the story hour. Although she thinks young people should be encouraged to read, she disapproves of their <u>immature</u> behavior.

Mrs. Wong is the head of the <u>adult</u> book section of the library. She is <u>middle-aged</u> and likes the <u>mature</u> company of adults. She likes to help older people find the books and information they need.

B. Mr. Copley works in the activities center of a retirement community. Many <u>old</u> people move to apartments in this community because it is a safe, quiet place to live. Mr. Copley likes helping the <u>elderly</u> people who live there. Even though they are <u>advanced in years</u>, many of them are <u>young at heart</u>. They enjoy many activities such as swimming, bowling, hiking, and dancing.

Betty Adelman used to participate in many activities. Mr. Copley enjoyed talking to her. Unfortunately, Mrs. Adelman has become <u>senile</u>. She can no longer remember things and can't concentrate for more than a few moments. Mr. Copley misses talking to her.

C. In the following conversation Megan, who is beginning her junior year in high school, is telling her mother about her new teachers.

Megan: It's going to be a long year, Mom. All of my teachers are <u>over the hill</u>. None of them is under thirty. Mr. Albertson, my English teacher, has gray hair and wrinkles!

Mother: Megan, watch what you're saying. You shouldn't talk about your teachers like that. Mr. Albertson might have gray hair and wrinkles, but that doesn't mean he's <u>past his prime</u>. Did his class sound interesting?

Megan: Well, I guess so. He said we'd study the lyrics of some rock songs because they are really poems. I guess that'll be okay.

Mother: Give him a chance, Megan. I think he'll surprise you.

IX. Exercises

Exercise 7: Beginning Practice

Add a word that is similar in meaning.

1. juvenile, youthful, _____

2. mature, grown-up, _____

3. on in years, old _____

4. childish, young, _____

Exercise 8: Word Choice

Choose the word or expression that best completes the sentence and then write it on the line.

1. This movie is for adults and not for children. It should only be seen by __?__ audiences. (*youthful, senile, mature*)

   1. _____

2. My grandparents are 70 years old but they are very active. They go to parties and like to play games with me. I like to visit them because they are so __?__ . (*mature, childlike, senile, young at heart*)

   2. _____

3. Nancy is 25 years old. She has a good job and just got her own apartment. Her parents are very proud of her because she is so __?__ . (*on in years, old, grown-up*)

   3. _____

4. During story hour a little girl asked the librarian a question. The librarian couldn't understand her because she spoke in a high __?__ voice. (*grown-up, elderly, childish*)

   4. _____

5. My father said that his new boss was __?__ . My mother said that it was not polite to talk about an older person like that. (*in her prime, mature, over the hill*)

   5. _____

6. That company likes to hire people who have worked for another company for several years. It wants employees who have experience and are __?__ . (*over the hill, immature, in their prime*)

   6. _____

7. Mr. Kowalski is 78. He often forgets things and can't find his way home. He is getting __?__ . (*juvenile, middle-aged, senile*)

   7. _____

8. Those children have been playing hockey for hours. I admire their __?__ energy. (*youthful, elderly, grown-up*)

   8. _____

Exercise 9: Rhyming Words

Complete the following rhymes by adding a word from the YOUNG–OLD domain that rhymes with (sounds the same as) the underlined word.

1. Some people come close to <u>tears</u>,
   When they realize they're __?__ in __?__ .

2. One thing I know for <u>sure</u>
   A five-year-old is __?__ .

3. To my daughter who's 16, I send this one <u>wish</u>:
   Please, stop acting so __?__ .

4. When you're 45 years old,
   It's the right <u>time</u>,
   To tell all your <u>friends</u>,
   That you're __?__ your __?__ .

1. _____ in _____

2. _____

3. _____

4. _____ your _____

Exercise 10: For Discussion

Once in a while, adults act like children. They might get angry too quickly or not do the work they are responsible for. We could call this <u>childish</u> behavior. <u>Childish</u> has a negative meaning in this sentence. But when a grown-up man has a smile like a little boy, we say that he has a <u>boyish</u> grin. <u>Boyish</u> has a positive meaning in this sentence. What happens when we use adjectives that normally describe young people to talk about old people? Why do you think they sometimes have a positive meaning and sometimes a negative one?

Discuss the following sentences. What do they mean? Do the adjectives for age have a positive or negative meaning?

1. I like to talk to my grandmother because she has such a <u>youthful</u> outlook on life.

2. At the party Steve made a fool of himself. He made <u>childish</u> remarks to the hostess and insulted several of the guests.

3. Earl's jokes are never very funny. He has a <u>juvenile</u> sense of humor.

4. Antonio is only 16, but he's a responsible person. He's very <u>grown-up</u> for his age.

5. Christine worked for the same company for several years, but last week she was fired. Her boss said that her <u>immature</u> behavior was the reason she was let go.

Exercise 11: Sense or Nonsense?

Decide whether each of the sentences below makes sense or is nonsense. Then circle the correct word.

1. She should be able to hike up to the top of that mountain. She's over the hill.   SENSE   NONSENSE

2. I always like to visit my grandmother. Even though she's 70 years old, she's still young at heart.   SENSE   NONSENSE

3. I enjoy being with children. They are always so elderly.	SENSE	NONSENSE
4. I think you should go to the concert with Jake. He seems to be a childish guy.	SENSE	NONSENSE
5. My 85-year-old uncle is senile so I really enjoy talking to him.	SENSE	NONSENSE
6. That singer should have retired years ago. Her performance was awful. She's definitely past her prime.	SENSE	NONSENSE
7. Many middle-aged people exercise regularly to stay in good shape.	SENSE	NONSENSE
8. He's really juvenile. Let's hire him for that important position.	SENSE	NONSENSE

Exercise 12: For Writing

Part A

Make a list of six of your relatives. You can include your mother, father, brothers, sisters, aunts, uncles, cousins, and grandparents. Then, choose an adjective and a noun from the domains you have just studied that best describe that person. Write them in the chart below.

Relative's Name	Adjective	Noun
1. _____	_____	_____
2. _____	_____	_____
3. _____	_____	_____
4. _____	_____	_____
5. _____	_____	_____
6. _____	_____	_____

Part B

Choose four of the people from the chart above. Write a short paragraph about each of them. In your paragraph, you should explain why the adjective and noun that you chose describe that relative.

Exercise 13: For Discussion or Writing

The title of this unit comes from an American movie, "It's a Wonderful Life." This movie tells the story of a man who is despondent because he thinks he made bad choices at different stages of his life.

Discuss or write about an important choice you or someone in your family made. At what stage of life was this choice made? How did this choice affect later stages of this person's life?

The answer to the "Riddle of the Sphinx" is a human being. A baby uses four "legs" when it crawls on its hands and knees, adults walk on two legs, and older people may use a cane, which is like a third leg.

Do It Yourself

CREATE YOUR OWN DOMAIN

I. Getting Ready

In a small group, discuss the following questions. During your discussions it may help to look back over some of the domains you have already studied.

1. What is a word domain?
2. What are some ways the words in a domain are related to each other? For example, <u>happy</u> is the opposite of <u>sad</u>, but <u>marching</u> is a kind of <u>walking</u>.
3. Which domains were the easiest to understand and learn? Which were the most difficult? Why?

II. Why Should You Do It Yourself?

In this unit you will work by yourself or with a partner to create your own domain. This will help you learn more new words because the words in your domain will become very familiar to you. Also, you will get a better understanding of how words are organized into domains. You will learn more about the structure of domains. This knowledge will help you in learning new words long after you have finished this book.

III. Creating Your Own Domain

Here are the steps to follow to create your own domain.

1. *Choose a Domain.* The first step in the process of creating a domain is to choose the words. Look at the six groups of words below and choose the group that is most interesting to you. Which group of words would you like to work with?

   Domain 1: bay, brook, cove, creek, gulf, harbor, inlet, lake, ocean, pond, pool, puddle, river, sea, sound, stream

Domain 2: affluent, badly off, broke, destitute, indigent, moneyed, needy, opulent, poor, rich, strapped, underprivileged, wealthy, well-heeled

Domain 3: catch sight of, examine, eyeball, gape at, gawk at, gaze at, glare at, glimpse, inspect, look at, observe, peer at, scrutinize, stare at, watch

Domain 4: city, downtown, ghetto, inner city, metropolis, metropolitan area, outskirts, slum, suburb, urban area

Domain 5: afraid, fearful, frightened, horrified, jumpy, nervous, panic-stricken, petrified, scared, scared stiff, skittish, terrified, uneasy, worried

Domain 6: advance, decline, decompose, deteriorate, fade, fail, get better, get worse, improve, look up, make progress, recover, recuperate, reform, relapse, sink

2. *Learn the Meanings of the Words.* The next step is to learn the meanings of the words in the domain you have chosen. First of all, you should look up each word in a good English dictionary. You can also ask other people (such as your teacher or native speakers of English) what the words mean to them. You should ask them to use the words in a sentence. Write down a definition of each word, using words you understand. If you hear your words being used in conversation or see them in writing, record those sentences as well. Be sure that you have several examples of how each word is used in a sentence.

3. *Organize the Words into a Chart of the Domain.* Analyze the information you have gathered so you can begin to organize the words. Your goal will be to put the words into a chart which is like the charts of the domains in the units you have studied so far.

   In order to do this, spend some time with your words. Think about their exact meanings. Are your words all similar in meaning? Are there some words are opposites? Go back and look at the domains in the units you have studied. Notice that some domains, such as WALK and TALK in Units 1 and 2, have several categories. Other domains, such as BEST–WORST in Unit 13, have only two basic categories. Can you put your words into a chart that is similar to one of the charts from this book?

4. *Write Some Exercises.* Your last task is to create two exercises for the words in your domain. You can look back at the units in this book to get ideas for the different types of exercises you might use. You can also create a new kind of exercise. Just remember that your exercises should help students learn the words from your domain.

IV. A Job Well Done

When you are finished, you should hand in to your teacher the following:

1. a chart for the words in your domain,
2. a list of the words in your domain, with their definitions and sample sentences, and
3. two exercises for the words in your domain.

Your teacher may want to use some of your domains and the exercises you have written to help the class learn more words.

V. Beyond Walk, Amble, Stroll

In this book you have learned many words grouped into many different word domains. But these are just a few of the domains there are in English. Now that you have had practice creating a domain, you should continue to use this important idea in your learning.

As you continue to study English, you are going to meet a lot of new words. Try to connect these new words to words you already know, by asking yourself some questions: Is this new word similiar to words I know? What are some opposites of this word? These questions will help you create your own word domains.

Creating domains can be an important way for you to learn more vocabulary on your own. It will keep your English vocabulary alive and growing.

Word Index

This word list contains the words presented in the domain charts in the units of this book. Unit references are given for each word. Words that are marked with an asterisk (*) are presented in the Expanding the Domain section of that unit.

A

a lot **9**
a mile a minute **3**
abhor **15**
abhorrence* **15**
abhorrent* **15**
abominable **13**
absorb **14**
accelerate **10**
acquire knowledge **14**
adolescence **17**
adolescent **17**
adorable* **15**
adoration* **15**
adore **15**
adult **17**
adulthood **17**
advance **18**
advanced in years **17**
affluent **18**
afraid **18**
all the time **9**
always **9**
amble **1**
ancient **16**
antique **16**
apartment **8**
appalling **13**
arid **12**
as a rule **9**
assemble **6**
assembler* **6**
assembly line worker* **6**
at a fast clip **3**
at a snail's pace **3**
at all times **9**
at full speed **3**
at full tilt **3**
at half speed **3**
at no time **9**
at times **9**
atrocious **13**
awesome **13**
awful **13**

B

babble **2**
baby **17**
bad **16**
badly off **18**
bark* **2**

bawl **5**
bay **18**
be crazy about **15**
be fond of **15**
be nuts about **15**
become bigger **10**
become smaller **10**
bed and breakfast* **8**
bellow **2**
bend someone's ear **2**
(the) best **13**
big **7**
birth **17**
blabber **2**
blabbermouth* **2**
blistering **11**
blizzard **12**
blow up **10**
blubber **5**
blue **4**
blue with cold **11**
boy **17**
boyhood **17**
boyish **17**
brand new **16**
breeze **12**
broaden **10**
broke **18**
broken-down **16**
broken-hearted* **4**
brook **18**
build **6**
builder* **6**
building* **6**
burst into tears **5**
burst out laughing **5**

C

cabin* **8**
cackle **5**
camper* **8**
can't stand **15**
care for **15**
castle **8**
catch sight of **18**
centenarian **17**
chat **2**
chatter **2**
chatterbox* **2**
cheerful **4**
cheery **4**

cherish **15**
chic **16**
child **17**
childhood **17**
childish **17**
childlike **17**
chilly **11**
chirp* **2**
chitchat **2**
chortle **5**
chuckle **5**
city **18**
climb **10**
coach **14**
coach* (*noun*) **14**
cold **11**
come up with **6**
commit to memory **14**
commonly **9**
conception **17**
condo **8**
condominium **8**
consistently **9**
constantly **9**
constrict **10**
construct **6**
construction worker* **6**
contemporary **16**
contented **4**
continually **9**
contract **10**
coo* **2**
cool **11**
cottage* **8**
cove **18**
create **6**
creation (beginning) **17**
creation* (something created) **6**
creator* **6**
creek **18**
creep **1**
cry **5**
cry one's eyes out **5**
cry over spilled milk* **5**
crybaby* **5**
current **16**
cyclone **12**

D

dated **16**
death **17**

decease **17**
decelerate **10**
decline **10, 18**
declining years **17**
decompose **18**
decrease **10**
decrepit **16**
deepen **10**
deflate **10**
delighted **4**
demise **17**
demonstrate **14**
demonstration* **14**
depressed **4**
despicable* **15**
despise **15**
despondent **4**
destitute **18**
deteriorate **18**
detest **15**
detestable* **15**
detestation* **15**
dig **15**
dilapidated **16**
dilute **10**
disapprove of **15**
disconsolate **4**
dislike **15**
double **10**
dowdy **16**
down **4**
down in the dumps **4**
downpour **12**
downtown **18**
dreadful **13**
drill **14**
drill* (*noun*) **14**
drizzle **12**
drought **12**
dry **12**
dump* **8**
duplex **8**
dwelling **8**
dwindle **10**

E

earthquake **12**
ecstatic **4**
edge **1**
educate **14**
education* **14**

educator* 14
efficiency 8
elated 4
elderly 17
enjoy 15
enjoyable* 15
enjoyment* 15
enlarge 10
enormous 7
erect 6
eruption 12
establish 6
establishment* 6
every now and then 9
every once in a while 9
every so often 9
examine 18
excellent 13
exceptional 13
expand 10
explain 14
explanation* 14
extraordinary 13
eyeball 18

F

fabulous 13
facilitate a discussion 14
facilitator* 14
fade 18
faded 16
fail 18
fall 10
fall off 10
falter 1
fantastic 13
fashionable 16
fast 3
fearful 18
feel affection for 15
feel an attraction for 15
feel tenderness for 15
fiery 11
find someone or something
    pleasant 15
first-class 13
first-rate 13
flood 12
flurry 12
fog 12
fortify 10
found 6
foundation* 6
founder* 6
freezing 11
freezing rain 12
frequently 9
fresh 16
frightened 18

frigid 11
from time to time 9
frosty 11

G

gab 2
gain knowledge 14
gale 12
gape at 18
gawk at 18
gaze at 18
generally 9
gentleman 17
get better 18
get bigger 10
get smaller 10
get worse 18
ghetto 18
giant 7
giant-sized 7
gigantic 7
giggle 5
girl 17
girlhood 17
girlish 17
give a lecture 14
glacial 11
glad 4
glare at 18
glimpse 18
gloomy 4
go down 10
go over 14
go up 10
gradually 3
grand 13
great 13
grin 5
grow 10
growl* 2
grown-up 17
grumble 2
grunt* 2
gulf 18
gust of wind 12

H

hail 12
happy 4
happy as a clam 4
happy as a lark 4
harbor 18
hardly ever 9
hasten 1
hastily 3
hate 15
hate someone's guts 15

hateful* 15
hatred* 15
have it in for 15
have no taste for 15
have no use for 15
haze 12
headlong 3
heartbroken 4
heavy-hearted* 4
heighten 10
high-rise 8
high-tech 16
high-technology 16
hiss* 2
hobble 1
holler 2
home 8
homeless shelter 8
horrendous 13
horrible 13
horrified 18
hot 11
hot as hell 11
hotel* 8
hotter than hell 11
house 8
housing project 8
hovel 8
howl* 2
howl (with laughter) 5
huge 7
humid 12
humidity 12
humongous 7
hurricane 12
hurriedly 3
hurry 1
hut 8

I

icy 11
idolize 15
igloo* 8
illustrate 14
illustration* 14
immature 17
immense 7
improve 18
in a bad mood* 4
in a flash 3
in a good mood* 4
in a jiffy 3
in general 9
in good spirits* 4
in hog heaven 4
in less than no time 3
in nothing flat 3
in one's prime 17
in seventh heaven 4

in slow motion 3
in style 16
in the doldrums 4
in the twinkling of an eye 3
in two shakes 3
in vogue 16
inch 1
inconsolable 4
increase 10
indigent 18
infancy 17
infant 17
infinitesimal 7
inflate 10
infrequently 9
inlet 18
inn* 8
inner city 18
innovative 16
inspect 18
instruct 14
instruction* 14
instructor* 14
invariably 9
invent 6
invention* 6
inventor* 6
irregularly 9
itsy-bitsy 7

J

jabber 2
joyful 4
joyous 4
jumpy 18
juvenile 17

K

kid 17

L

lady 17
lake 18
large 7
laugh 5
laugh out loud 5
lead a discussion 14
leader* 14
learn 14
learn about 14
learn by heart 14
lecture 14
lecturer* 14

leisurely 3
lengthen 10
lickety-split 3
lightning 12
light-hearted* 4
likable* 15
like 15
like a blue streak 3
like mad 3
liking* 15
limp 1
little 7
little by little 3
loathe 15
loathsome* 15
loathing* 15
look at 18
look up 18
lousy 13
lovable* 15
love 15
low 4
low-down 13
low-income public
    housing 8
lukewarm 11
luxury apartment 8
luxury condominium 8

M

macro-* 7
magnificent 13
make 6
make progress 18
maker* 6
man 17
manhood 17
mansion 8
manufacture 6
manufacturer* 6
march 1
marvelous 13
master 14
mature 17
maxi-* 7
melancholy 4
memorization* 14
memorize 14
metropolis 18
metropolitan area 18
microscopic 7
micro-* 7
middle-aged 17
miniature 7
miniscule 7
mini-* 7
minor 17
minute 7
miserable 4

mist 12
model (*verb*) 14
model* (*noun*) 14
modern 16
moldy 16
moneyed 18
monstrous 7
more often than not 9
morning, noon, and night 9
motel* 8
moth-eaten 16
mournful* 4
muggy 12
multiple-family dwelling 8
multiply 10
mumble 2
murmur 2
mutter 2

N

narrow 10
natural disaster 12
needy 18
nervous 18
never 9
new 16
night and day 9
no good 13
no way* 9
no way, José* 9
nosedive 10
not care for 15
not ever 9
not in a million years* 9
not on your life* 9
not under any circum-
    stances 9
not under any condition 9
now and again 9
now and then 9
numb with cold 11

O

object to 15
observe 18
obsolescent 16
obsolete 16
occasionally 9
ocean 18
octogenarian 17
often 9
old 16, 17
old age 17
old-fashioned 16
old-timer 17
on cloud nine 4

on every occasion 9
on in years 17
on no occasion 9
on occasion 9
on the cutting edge 16
on the double 3
on top of the world 4
once in a while 9
opulent 18
ordinarily 9
organization* 6
organize 6
organizer* 6
origin 17
outdated 16
outmoded 16
outskirts 18
outstanding 13
out-of-this-world 13
over the hill 17
overjoyed 4

P

pace 1
palace 8
panic-stricken 18
passing away 17
passing on 17
past one's prime 17
peer at 18
perfect 13
petite 7
petrified 18
pick up 14
piece together 6
pint-sized 7
piping hot 11
place* 8
pleased 4
plod 1
plummet 10
plunge 10
pond 18
pool 18
poor 18
practice 14
precipitation 12
present 14
presentation* 14
presenter* 14
pre-adolescent 17
pre-teen 17
prime of life 17
prize 15
produce 6
producer* 6
product* 6
prowl 1

puberty 17
puddle 18
purr* 2
put together 6
put up 6

Q

quadruple 10
quick as a wink 3
quickly 3

R

rain 12
rain buckets* 12
rain cats and dogs* 12
rain pitchforks and hammer
    handles* 12
raindrop 12
rainstorm 12
ramble 1
rancid 16
rapidly 3
rarely 9
rattle on 2
recent 16
recover 18
recuperate 18
red hot 11
reduce 10
reform 18
regularly 9
reinforce 10
relapse 18
repeatedly 9
residence 8
revere 15
reverence* 15
review 14
rich 18
rise 10
river 18
roam 1
roar 2
roar with laughter 5
rotten 13, 16
routinely 9
rowhouse 8
run off at the mouth 2
run-down 16
rusty 16

S

sad 4
saunter 1

scalding 11
scarcely ever 9
scared 18
scared stiff 18
scorching 11
scream 2
scrutinize 18
sea 18
seldom 9
senile 17
senior citizen 17
sensational 13
set up 6
shabby 16
shack 8
shanty 8
shed tears 5
shoot up 10
shorten 10
shout 2
show someone how to 14
shower 12
shriek 2
shriek with laughter 5
shrink 10
shuffle 1
single-family dwelling 8
sink 18
sizzling 11
skittish 18
skyrocket 10
sleet 12
slink 1
slouch 1
slow down 10
slowly 3
sluggishly 3
slum 18
small 7
smile 5
smirk 5
smog 12
snarl* 2
sneak 1
snicker 5
snow 12
snowflake 12
snow flurry 12
snowfall 12
snowstorm 12
soar 10
sob 5
somber 4
sometimes 9
sorrowful* 4
sound 18
spectacular 13
speed up 10
speedily 3
splendid 13

spoiled 16
sporadically 9
sprinkle 12
squeal* 2
stagger 1
stale 16
stare at 18
state-of-the-art 16
steal 1
steamy 11, 12
step by step 3
stone cold 11
strapped 18
stream 18
strengthen 10
stride 1
stroll 1
strut 1
studio 8
stumble 1
stylish 16
suburb 18
sunny 4
super 13
superb 13
superior 13
swagger 1
swiftly 3

T

take a dislike to 15
take a nosedive 10
talk 2
taper off 10
tattered 16
teach 14
teacher* 14
teen 17
teenage years 17
teenager 17
teeny 7
teepee* 8
tenement 8
tepid 11
terrible 13
terrific 13
terrified 18
the best 13
the worst 13
think of 6
think up 6
threadbare 16
thrilled 4
thunder 12
thunderstorm 12
tickled pink 4
tidal wave 12
tiny 7

tiptoe 1
titter 5
toddle 1
toddler 17
topnotch 13
tornado 12
tot 17
townhouse 8
train 14
trainer 14
treasure 15
triple 10
trudge 1
tutor 14
tutor* (*noun*) 14
twilight of life 17
twister 12
twitter* 2
typhoon 12

U

underprivileged 18
uneasy 18
unhappy 4
unhurriedly 3
up 4
upbeat 4
up-to-date 16
urban area 18
usually 9

V

van* 8
very big 7
very little 7
very small 7
villa 8
volcano 12

W

waddle 1
wail 5
walk 1
walking on air 4
wander 1
warm 11
watch 18
water down 10
weaken 10
wealthy 18
weep 5
well-heeled 18
when hell freezes over* 9

whimper 5
whisper 2
white-hot 11
widen 10
wind 12
windstorm 12
wintry 11
without fail 9
woman 17
womanhood 17
wonderful 13
worn-down 16
worn-out 16
worried 18
worship 15
(the) worst 13
wretched 13